EPITAPHS

IN THE

OLD BURIAL PLACE,

DEDHAM, MASS.

Copied and Arranged

BY

Rev. CARLOS SLAFTER, A. M.

PUBLISHED BY
THE DEDHAM HISTORICAL SOCIETY.
1888.

Notice

In many older books, foxing (or discoloration) occurs and, in some instances, print lightens with wear and age. Reprinted books, such as this, often duplicate these flaws, notwithstanding efforts to reduce or eliminate them. The pages of this reprint have been digitally enhanced and, where possible, the flaws eliminated in order to provide clarity of content and a pleasant reading experience.

Epitaphs in the Old Burial Place,
Dedham, Mass.

Originally published
Dedham, Massachusetts
1888

Reprinted by:

Janaway Publishing, Inc.
732 Kelsey Ct.
Santa Maria, California 93454
(805) 925-1038
www.janawaygenealogy.com

2010

ISBN 10: 1-59641-194-5
ISBN 13: 978-1-59641-194-4

Made in the United States of America

THE OLDEST TOMBSTONE NOW STANDING
IN THE CEMETERY.

THE ANCIENT BURIAL PLACE OF DEDHAM.

THE EPITAPHS UPON THE TOMB STONES.

In every old Massachusetts town, among the localities of special interest, is the spot where the early inhabitants committed to the earth the bodies of their lamented dead. Consecrated anew year after year by the tears of love and sorrow, it becomes hallowed ground; and as we bend over the low headstone and decipher its quaint inscription, we are reminded of the affection which erected it, and which still commends it to our respect and care. We are told by the humblest stone that a loved one had died, and that loving ones survived who desired to honor, and preserve, the memory of the dead. It is indeed a brief story; but it is a story which we love to read, though its age may be reckoned in centuries. So our old cemetery is a record of human affection well fitted to improve the heart and stir the imagination. It is not necessarily a gloomy spot. It speaks rather of rest and peace after the labors and turmoil of life are ended.

We have endeavored to ascertain *how early*, and *where*, the original burial place of Dedham was located. The town records do not answer these questions directly, but they do enable us to form a definite opinion on the subject. Ezechiell Holliman, the original Baptist who baptised Roger Williams, is spoken of in the town records, under date of Dec. 31, 1636, as follows: "And for that Ezechiell Holliman hath felled one great Timber tree for clapboard, without his owne lott, contrary to an order made in that behalfe, therefore, he is fined to pay unto the collector, for the use of the towne, the sum of ten shillings." From this it is evident that Holliman had a lot in his possession as early as 1636. Now, in the grant to him, that lot is described as follows: "Twelve acres more or less as lyeth between the way (now Court street) leading from the Keye to the Pond towards the east and Nicholas Phillips towards the west, and butts upon the said way wynding towards the north, *and the way leading to the burying pl ice towards the south.*"

From this we see that in 1636 there was a "waye" leading to the burying place. This "waye" probably passed between where now stand the house of Mrs. Benjamin Adams and St. Paul's church, and also passed over the ground recently purchased by the town of Mrs. Adams and added to the cemetery.

Having thus located the road to the "burying place," we find the "burying place" itself by the following description of the lot granted to Nicholas Phillips: "Twelve acres more or less, as it lyeth betweene Ezechiel Holliman towards the east, & Lambert Genere towards the west. And butts upon Charles River towards the north & upon the Swampe & '*burying place towards the South.*'" Thus it appears that the primitive "burying place" was *south* of Nicholas Phillips' lot, and was approached by a road south of Holliman's.

But Holliman's lot embraced the land on which now stand the Orthodox, the Unitarian, and the Episcopal churches; while Phillips' lot is now partly occupied by the county prison. Therefore we conclude that the ground first used for interments was a small, oblong piece, beginning near where the ministers' monument now stands, and extending some distance westerly. Such a lot would be south of the Phillips land, and would be approached by a "waye" south of Holliman's. Why this place was chosen we are not informed, but it is a reasonable supposition that it was open land, perhaps an Indian cornfield, and therefore suitable and convenient for immediate use.

When was the first person buried in this ground? The earliest death mentioned in Dedham records occurred in 1637. But it seems improbable that a burial place should be located before anybody had died. When the first death occurred, then, the question of a place of burial would first present itself, and then the whole body of proprietors in the town would decide upon the appropriate spot. Probably the first year of the settlement, 1635, did not pass before some yielded to the hardships and casualties to which colonists in an unsubdued wilderness are exposed, and were buried in that ground.

It would be reasonable to assume that the death rate, especially among children, was large, on account of a lack of necessary care and comforts. Consequently it was soon apparent that the first little burial lot would be found inadequate to the wants of the town, and, in 1638, Joseph Kingsbury, who had come into possession of the lot of Ezechiell Holliman, and Nicholas Phillips exchanged, for other lands in the town, a portion of their land at the south end of their lots, to enlarge the accommodation for the dead.

After the building of the church, or about 1639, a "bearing waye," one rod wide, was laid out where Bullard street now is, and led directly from the church, and entered the burying ground at its northwest corner. It is probable that the road leading to the south side of the burying ground was then, or soon afterwards, discontinued.

The boundaries of the burial place, thus enlarged, continued the same for about 175 years. They included an area of about one acre. For a period of one hundred years, this was the only place of burial in the town, and it is needless to say that some parts of it were dug over several times to furnish graves for successive generations. Where a stone was not set up, the place of interment was soon forgotten, and so received another occupant. I think we should be surprised to know how many bodies were buried in that acre of ground. Of course we never can know, but from the nature of things, several thousands have there found their last resting place, and their dust has been commingled more rudely than one would care to know.

Every one must feel that hereafter "*The old burying ground*" ought to be tenderly cared for, as the final resting place of many noble men and women. One after another, for nearly two hundred years, they were gathered to that little acre of ground, approaching it through that narrow "bearing-way," and, in most cases, conveyed thither by the strong and kindly arms of their neighbors. There let them rest undisturbed, and let not the graves of strangers invade any more the little space which they have so long occupied. It is to be remembered that in every foot of that soil is mingled the dust of those who by their labors changed this town from a savage wilderness to a spot where comfort and refinement rejoice to dwell. As the ashes of thousands are accumulated there, with no monuments to distinguish one from another, it is truly fitting that the most beautiful trees of the forest should weave a canopy over their common resting place, and that the unbroken turf, starred with the daisy and the buttercup, should symbolize their calm and honored repose.

DIAGRAM OF THE BURIAL PLACE.

WEST.

EARLY ADDITION.

Main Entrance. Bullard Street.

Range	South name		North name	Count
XIX	1 Dyer		Richards	54
XVIII	1 Hayward		Richards	40
XVII	1 Stowell		Willson	36
XVI	1 Stone		Whiting	38
XV	1 Musche		Bullard	23
XIV	1 Bullard		Bickford	51
XIII	1 Johnson		Badlam	22
XII	1 Whiting		Parker	29
XI	1 Strong		Howe	34
X	1 Gay		Carter	21
IX	1 Gay		Cooper	27
VIII	1 Faulkner	to	Pond	25
VII	1 Baker	to	Kelton	21
VI	1 Guild	to	Whiting	24
V	1 Nichols	to	Balch	17
IV	1 Keith	to	Farrington	11
III	1 Whiting	to	Whiting	16
II	1 Arbonne	to	Dowse	23
I	1 Cobb	to	Nicholson	9

NEWEST ADDITION. SOUTH. Village Avenue. NORTH.

EAST.

ST. PAUL'S CHURCH GROUNDS.

This diagram represents the old Burial Place, and is designed to aid one in finding the stones which bear the Epitaphs. The nineteen spaces represent divisions of the ground, which are called *Ranges*. The Roman numerals indicate where stones are set along the south side of the Burial Place, to show where the Ranges begin. The number of gravestones, or monuments, in each Range is shown by figures at the right side of the diagram. In the *Special Index* each name is followed by a Roman numeral and an Arabic number: these refer to its Range and Number in the Record, and also serve to show its approximate position in the Burial Place. The stones in each Range are numbered from *south* to *north* in the record; and although there are some irregularities in their position, it is hoped that a little patience will enable a person to find any one of them.

FIRST PARISH.

SPECIAL INDEX

To the Epitaphs in the Ancient Burial Place.

ABRAHAM, Elizabeth, ix, 26. ADAMS, Sarah J., x, 7; William, xv, 4. ALBERT, — —, xi, 14. ALDEN, Adeline. xvi, 32; George, viii, 6; Hannah, viii, 9; Leonard, xvi, 32. ALGER, Betsey E., xvi, 2. ALLIN; John, xv, 4. ALLWRIGHT, Alfred, x, 8. ARBONNE, Charlotte, ii, 1. ATHERTON, Abner, xvi, 17; Betsey, xvi, 17; Catherine, xvi, 17. AVERY, Bethia, xiv, 29; Daniel, xiv, 29; Elizabeth, xiv, 4; Jerusha, xiv, 29; Jonathan, xiv, 29; Lucy, xiv, 29; Mary, xv, 5; Robert, xiv, 5; xiv, 6; William, ix. 2; xiv, 29; xiv, 29, xiv, 29; xiv, 29; xiv, 29; xv, 6.

BADLAM, Lemuel, xiii, 21; Lydia, xiii. 22; Polly, xiii, 20; Rebecca, xiii, 18; William, xiv, 46. BAKER,Abigail, xviii, 23; Anne E., vi, 2; Chloe, vii, 12; Daniel, vii, 20; Eliphalet, vii, 1; Elizabeth, iii, 2; Hannah, xvii, 33; John, vii, 5; xviii. 22; Joseph, xvii, 33; Mary, vii, 19; Nathaniel, vii, 1; vii, 1; xviii, 21; Patty E., vii, 5; Seth, xviii, 24. BALCH, William. v, 17. BARROWS, Edward. xix, 46; Elizabeth, xix, 46; Thomas, xix, 46; xix, 46. BARTON, Janet. xix, 6. BATES, Joshua, xv, 4; Mary F., xiii, 14; Samuel, iii, 5. BATTLE, Ebenezer, vii, 11. BEDELL, Lucy E., x, 11. BETCHER, Joseph, xv, 4. BERRY, Caroline, xi, 28; James, xi, 31; John, xi, 28; Martha, xi, 30. BICKFORD, Willard T., xiv, 51. BINGHAM, Almira, xiii, 6; Daniel, xiii, 6; Jerusha A., xiii, 6; Pliny, xiii, 6. BIRD, Catherine, xviii, 10; Samuel, xviii, 10; Walter F., xvii, 14. BISSETT, Charles, xix, 19; Maria I., xix, 20. BONNEMORT, George P., xix, 53; Maratio N., xix, 53; Mariatho N., xix, 53; Mary G., xix, 53; Nicholas, xix, 53; Nicholas M., xix, 53. BONNY, Deborah, xii, 3. BOSWORTH, Asaph, xiv, 30. BOWERS, Lewis, xii, 15. BOYNTON, Abigail, xix, 43; Jesse P., xix, 43; John, xix, 43; Luther, xix, 43. BRACKET, Nathaniel, xii, 17. BROWN, Charles H., xix, 33; Eliza A., ix, 23; ix, 25; George, ix, 24; Martha, viii, 9; Sarah, ix, 21; William F., ix, 22. BULLARD, Abba, xv, 20; Charles, xvi, 33; Elizabeth, xiv, 2; Grace, xix, 30; Harriet, xvii, 11; xvii, 11; Isaac, xv, 22; xix, 30; Jesse, xvii, 11; John, xv, 21; Lydia, xvi, 34; Mary. xix, 31; Patience, xv, 23; Susan, xvii, 11; Willard, xvii, 11; William, xiv, 1; xiv, 3; xvi, 34. BURGESS. Abbie P., xvi, 31; Carrie F., xvi, 31. BUTRICK, Eliza J., xvi, 2.

CAIN, Elizabeth, vi, 5; John E. M., vi, 5; John P., vi, 5. CALDWELL, Mary, xviii, 8. CARTER, Harriet, x, 21. CHAMBERLAIN, Albion E., xi, 26. CHANDLER, Benjamin W., xix, 22; Eliza J., xix, 22. CHISHOLM, George, xix, 6; Isabel, xix, 6; William, xix, 6. CLAPP, Betsey D., x, 10; Charles W., x, 10; Elizabeth D., x, 10; Henry F., x, 10; Jane D., x, 10; x, 10; Jesse, x, 10; John D., x, 10; x, 10; x, 10; Mary, x, 10; Mary A., x, 10; x, 10; Mary B., x, 10. CLARK, Abigail A., x, 20; Elvira R., xix, 26; Horatio, xix, 26; Spencer W., xvii, 4. COBB, Calvin, xvi, 28; Jonathan H., i, 1; Sophia D., i, 1. COBHAM, Josiah, xvii, 7. COBURN, Alvan, x, 14; x, 15; Hiram, x, 14; x, 15. CODDING, Adelbert A., xiii, 7. COL. BURN, Annah xix, 16; Benjamin, xvi, 24; George L., xvii, 24; Jesse, xix, 16; John, xix, 16; Rebekah, xiv, 16. COLMAN, Benjamin, xix, 17. COOLIDGE, Horace, xix, 45. COOPER, Ann, ix, 27; Samuel, ix, 27. CRANE, Hannah, xi, 33. CROOKER, Gerty, xviii, 7. CROSBY, Edmund, xiv, 7; Fanny M., xviii, 16; Heman, xviii, 16; Mary, xviii, 16; Obed S., xviii, 16; Rachel A., xiv, 7; Rhoda, xviii, 16; Turana, xviii, 16. CUMMINGS, Polly, xv, 10. CURRIEA, Caroline S., vi, 3. CURTIS, Hannah, xv, 9.

DAMON, Hopestill, xvii, 34; John, xiv. 49; Mary, xvii, 34. DANIELL, Jesse, xvii, 25; Josiah, xviii, 38; Mary, xvii, 25; Nabby, xviii, 37; Nancy S., xvii, 25;

Timothy, xviii, 35. DAVIS, Washington, ix, 20. DAY, Prudence, vii, 9. DEAN, Betsey, xi, 9; Elizabeth B., xv, 16; Hannah, xv, 12; John, xi, 9; xi, 11; Joseph, xv, 12; Josiah, xv, 16; Louis E., xv, 11; Mary, ix, 5; xi, 10; xv, 16; Mary A., xv, 14. DEWIN, Margaret, ii, 3. DEWOLF, Hannah, xvii, 17; Nathan, xvii, 18. DEXTER, Samuel, xv, 4; ——, vi, 17. DICKERMAN, Anna, xvi, 32. DIX, Nathaniel F., xiv, 34. DOGGETT, Samuel, x, 9. DONLEY, Francis, xix, 10. DOWSE, Edward, ii, 23; Sarah, ii, 23. DRAKE, Polly, xvii, 3; Sarda, xvii, 3. DRAPER, Abigail, viii, 15; Abijah, vii, 14; vii, 16; ix, 13; Alice, viii, 17; Desire, viii, 19; Dorothy, xi, 15; Ebenezer, v, 6; xi, 15; James, viii, 15; Lucy C., viii, 18; Lydia, iv. 5; Sybil A., xi, 15. DUDLEY, Harriet, xix, 13. DUNTIN, Ruth, xiv, 38. DURANT, Faith, xi, 24; Rachel, xi. 25. DWIGHT, Mary, xix, 24; Timothy, xiii, 4. DYAR, Hannah, xix, 1.

EATON, Abby M., viii, 9; Abigail, viii, 9; Calvin, v, 17; Desire, vi, 2; vii, 4; Eliza, viii, 9; Hannah, viii, 9; Isaac, v, 17; v, 17; J. Ellis, viii, 9; Joel, viii, 9; John, vi, 2; vii, 3; viii, 9; viii, 9; John E., viii, 9; Lucy, viii, 9; viii, 9; viii, 9; Luther, viii. 9; viii, 9; Maria, viii, 9; Rebecca, vi, 2; Sarah, v, 17. EDSON, Betsey, xiv, 47; Robert, xiv, 44; ——, xiv, 45. ELLIS, Betsey, ix, 6; George, ix, 7; Jesse, ix, 7; Joseph, xvi, 6; Lucy, ix, 7; Lyman, x, 13; Samuel, ix, 4. EVERETT, John, xix, 30.

FAIRBANKS, Calvin, iii, 4; iv, 3; iv, 4; Ebenezer, i, 2; ii,2; Jason, iii, 3; Mary, i, 3; Prudence, i, 4; i, 5. FALES, Charles S., viii, 10; David, iii, 13, Elizabeth, xii, 28; Mary, iii, 13; xi. 26; Mary L., viii, 11; Nathaniel, ii, 17; Nehemiah, xi, 26; xii, 27; Rebecca, ii, 17; xvi, 32; Samuel, xvi, 32; Sarah, xii, 27; Stephen, viii, 11; Timothy, xiii, 17. FARMER, George P., xii, 16. FARRINGTON, Abby M., xi, 5; Abner, iv, 8; Benjamin, xi, 20; Charlotte, xiv, 43; Desire, xi, 20; Ebenezer, iv, 9; iv, 10; Eliphalet, xi, 20; Elizabeth, iv, 10; Hannah, iv, 7; James, xi, 20; Lucy, xiv, 42; Lucy P., xi, 20; Mehitable, v, 5; Oscar E., xi, 6; Sarah, xi, 20; Simeon, xi, 20; Stephen, xiv, 40; William, xiv, 41; ——, iv, 11. FAULKNER, Elizabeth W., viii, 1. FELTON, Charles C., xviii, 12; Horace, xviii, 12; Mary W., xviii, 12; Rosilla A., xviii, 11. FESSENDEN, George, vii, 2; John, vii, 2; Nancy B., vii, 2. FISH, Abbie B., xvi, 8; xvi, 8; Ebenezer, xvi, 8; xvi, 8; Eli, xvi, 8; Frances M., xvi, 8; James F., xvi, 8; Sarah H., xvi, 8; Susan F., xvi, 8. FISHER, Billings, xvi, 19; Daniel, xviii, 13; Hannah, xvi, 19; Hannah M., xvi, 19; Joseph, xiii, 15; Josiah, vi, 18; vi, 19; xiii, 16; Lavina, xiv, 34; Margaret, xvi, 4; Mary, xiii, 10; Nathaniel, xix, 23; Paul, xiv, 34; Rebecca, v, 16. FORD, Agnes, xviii, 2; John, xviii, 2. FORIST, Belinda, xii, 11. Fox, Thomas, xv, 7. FRANK, —. —., xi, 14. FROST, John H., xvi, 18. FULLER, Enoch, xvi, 29; Hezekiah, xvi, 27; Judith, iii, 10; x, 3.

GAY, Daniel, ii, 9; ii, 10; Ebenezer, ii, 7; Elizabeth, x, 1; Hezekiah, xiii, 13; John, x, 2; Joseph; ix, 18; Josiah; ii, 4; Jotham, xix, 50; Lusher, ix, 16; Lydia, ix, 1; xix, 52; Mary, i, 6; ix, 8; ix, 15; x, 2; Moses, ii, 5; Phebe, ix, 19; Sarah, ii, 6; ii, 8; ix, 17; x, 4. GOULD, John, xix, 38. GRAHAM, Lydia, xix, 8; Lydia C., xix, 8. GRANT, Caleb, xi, 3. GRIGGS, James, xiii, 3. GUILD, Abner, xix, 14; Alfred R., vi, 2; Catherine, iii, 8; George R., xix, 14; Henrietta, xix, 14; John, vi, 2; Joseph, iii, 7; Miranda, vi, 2; Miriam, iii, 6; Nathaniel, vi, 1; vi, 2; Sophia, xix, 14; Sophia H., xix, 14. GUPTILL, Lizzie M., xix, 7.

HALL, Amos, xi, 16; Sabina, xi, 16. HAMMER, William P., vi, 11. HAPGOOD, Adeline R., ii, 22; Catherine A., ii, 22; Catherine C., ii, 22; Henry ii, 22; Henry M., ii, 22; Lucy A., ii, 22. HARGRAVES, Lucy A., xvi, 2. HAVEN, Jason, xv, 4. HAWS, Sebiah, xix, 11. HAYWARD, Mary, xviii, 1. HERRING, Ann, x, 12; Sarah, xviii, 25. HIRSCH, George S., xv, 3. HOLMES, Eliza G., xii,

FIRST PARISH. 11

13. HOPKINS, Benjamin, xviii, 17; Esther, xviii. 17; Harriet H., xviii. 18.
HOUGHTON, C. E., xiv, 33; Charles L., xiv, 31; C. L., xiv, 33; E., xiv, 33; Jesse, xi, 4; P., xiv, 33; W^m., xiv, 33. HOWE, Anne, xi, 32; Calvin, xvii, 28; Calvin N., xvii, 27; Isaac, xi, 32; Isaac F., xi, 32; xi, 32; Nancy H., xi, 27; Polly, xvii, 29; Thomas, xi, 34. HUMPHREY, Sarah, iii, 12. HURST, William, xix, 25. HUTCHINS, George, xii, 9; George II., xii, 8; Joseph, xii, 9; Sarah, xii, 9.

IVERS, Caroline F., xvi, 30; Samuel, xvi, 30.

JACKMAN, Martha, xviii, 6. JACKSON, Lucy, xv, 15. JOHNSON, Alfred, xvi, 2; Annie L.; xvi, 2; Elizabeth, xiii, 1; John, xiii, 2; Lucy A., xvi, 2; Noel M., xvi, 2.

KAHLMEYER, Henry C., xii, 4. KEITH, Chloe, iv, 1. KELTON, Catharine A., vii, 21. KINGSBURY, Abigail, xii, 7; Elizabeth, x, 17; Eliza C., xi, 15; Ezekiel, xi, 15; George, vii, 10; Hannah, x, 16; Joseph, vii, 8; Martha T., xi, 15; Mary, vii, 7; Mary D., xi, 15; Nathaniel, x, 18; xii, 6; Noah, xiii, 8; Sarah, vii, 10.

LAMSON, Alvan, xv, 4. LANE, Hannah S., xii, 5. LEWIS, Abigail, vi, 7; Anna, ii, 21; Asa, ii, 20; Eunice, ii, 19; Helena M., viii, 14; Joseph, vi, 8; Levi C., viii, 14; Lydia J., viii, 13; Margaret A., viii, 13; Mary O., xii, 12; Molly, vi, 9; Paul, ii, 18; Sally, vi, 10; Samuel, ii, 21. LIEBOLD, Caroline, vi, 13; George J., vi, 12. LUCE, Charley A., iv, 2. LYONS, Mary, xvii, 8; Mary J., xvii, 8.

MABBETT, Florence L., xix, 2. MACKERWETHY, Hannah, x, 19. MACOMBER, Samuel, xii, 10. MARSH, Charles, ix, 3; Elizabeth, ix, 3; Francis, ix, 3; Henry, ix, 3; John, ix, 3; Martin, ix, 3; ix, 3; ix, 3; Martin M., ix, 3. MASON, Abigail, iii, 9; iv, 6; Anne, iv, 6; Eliphalet F., xiii, 14; George E., xiii, 14; xiii, 14; John, iv, 6; xvi, 36; Mary F., xiii, 14; Rhoda, vi, 14; Thaddeus, iv, 6; Thaddeus II., iv, 6. MAY, Augustus R., xi, 15; Catharine K., xi, 15; Daniel, xi, 15. MAYO, Abigail, xix, 9; James, xix, 9. McWHIRK, John, xvii, 10. MESSENGER, Henry, i, 8; John, ii, 11; Newton, ii, 12; Olive, i, 7. METCALF, Augusta L., xiv, 14; Elias, xiv, 11; Elizabeth, xiv, 19; Grace, xiv, 23; Hannah S., xiv, 13; John, xiv, 20; John S., xiv, 16; Jonathan, xiv, 10; xiv, 26; Joseph, xiv, 12; xiv, 24; xiv, 27; Katharine, xiv, 21; Lyman A., xiv, 15; Rebecca, xiv, 27; Reuben, xiv, 13; Ruth, xiv, 24; Samuel, xiv, 8; Sarah, xiv, 22; Thomas, xiv, 9; xiv, 17; xiv, 18; Timothy, xiv, 25. MOODY, Eliezer, xix, 21. MORRELL, Abner, xiv, 35; Eliakim, xiv, 35; Isaac, xiv, 35; Joseph, xiv, 35; Nancy, xiv, 35; Nancy W., xiv, 35; Ruth, xiv, 35. MORSE, Harriet, viii, 5; James, viii, 7; Lewis, xix, 12; Lucy. viii, 8; Nancy W., viii, 6; Ruth S., xix, 12; Silas, xix, 12. MUSCHE, Isabella, xv, 1.

NASON, Clarissa H., xvii, 9. NEWELL, Ebenezer, xix, 40; xix, 41. NICHOLS. Abel, v, 1. NICHOLSON, Elizabeth R., i, 9; Maria, i, 9, NOYES, Catherine, xv, 13; Hannah, xv, 13; xv, 13; Mary A., xv, 10; Nancy G., xv, 10; Nathaniel, xv, 13; Otis, xv, 10.

ONION, Joseph, xiv, 50. OSGOOD, Maria, xix, 34.

PAINE, Fannie A., xix, 37. PARKER, Alexander A., v, 8; Catharine, v, 7; Jonathan, xii, 29; Sarah, x, 5. PARTRIDGE, Angelina, xix, 3; Sarah G., xix, 3. PAUL, Abby P., vii, 13; Abigail, vi, 21; vi, 21; xi, 23; Ebenezer, vi, 20; vi, 21; Hannah, xii, 14; Hiram, xix, 18; Isaac, vi, 21; Lydia, vi, 21; Martha, vii, 13; Mary, vi, 4; Samuel, vi, 21; vii, 13; xi, 22; Susan B., xix, 18; Susan F., vii, 13; William, vi, 4; xvi, 32. PENNIMAN, George R., xviii, 30; Henry A., xviii, 28; James, xviii, 29; Sally F., xviii, 28. PHILLIPS, Francis, xii, 26; Mehitable, xii, 26; Nathan, xii, 26. PIERSON, Jacob, vii, 6. POLLARD, Jonathan, xv, 19. POMEROY, Arabella, xiv, 30; George, xiv, 39. POND, Abigail, xviii, 34; Charles

D., vii, 16; Eliphalet, vii, 17; vii, 17; vii, 17; Elizabeth, vii, 17; viii, 22; Flora M., vii. 16; Henry E., vii, 17; Julia A., vii, 17; Mary E., vii, 16; Nathaniel D., vii, 16; Prudence, vii, 17; Rebecca, viii, 21; Sally, xviii, 34; xviii, 34; William A., vii, 17; viii, 25. POYEN, Louis F., xvi, 2. PRESCOTT, Mary E., xi, 16; Sabina T., xi, 16.

REDHOUGH, Elizabeth A., viii. 12; James W., viii, 12. RICHARDS, Abby F., xix, 34; Abiathar, xiii, 9; xvi, 22; xix, 48; Albert A., xii, 22: Alvin, xii, 25; Betsey, vi, 15; Catharine, xvi, 23; Danford; vi, 15; Ebenezer, xviii, 39; Edward, xvi, 10; xvi, 26; Eliphalet, xix, 51; Eliza, vi, 15; Elizabeth, xvi. 21; xix, 47; xix, 49; Emily C., xiii, 9; Fanny, xiii, 9; Frank, xiii, 9; Franklin D., xiii, 9; xiii, 9; Hannah, vi, 15; xvi, 25; xvii,31; Hephzibah, xix, 35; Horace, xiii, 9; Irving W., xix, 34; James, xvii, 31; John, xviii, 40; Jonathan, xvii, 30; Joseph, xi, 12; Luther, xii, 24; Martin, xii, 23; Mary, xi, 12; xix, 54; Mason, vi, 15; Nathaniel, xvi, 3; xvii, 26; Olive M., vi, 15; Phebe W., vi, 15; Polly B., xii, 24; Rebecca, xiv, 32; Reuel, xvi, 20; Roxana, vi, 15; Roxana L., vi, 15; Sally, v, 14; Samuel, vi, 15; Sarah, xvi, 5; xviii, 40; Seth, vi, 15; Thaddeus, xvi, 9; Thankful, xviii, 30. RITZ, Maria C., xviii, 4. ROBERTS, Nancy, viii, 2. ROBINSON, Deborah C., xviii, 27; Esther, xviii, 27; Melissa, xviii, 27.

SAMPSON, Cynthia, xix, 18; Mary, xix, 15. SCARBOROUGH, Elizabeth, xi, 13. SCHOPF, Barbara, xvii, 6. SEARS, Lydia, xiii, 19. SHAW, Hannah, ii, 23; Samuel, ii, 23. SHUMWAY; Alvin J., xvii, 25; Erastus, xvii, 25; Erastus D., xvii, 25; Mary, xvii, 25. SHUTTLEWORTH, Hannah, xviii, 9; Henry, xviii, 9; Jeremiah, xviii, 9; xviii, 9; Samuel, xviii, 9; Sukey, xviii, 9. SMALL, Ahira, xii, 19; Betsey, xii, 20; Ellen M., xii, 18; Jane E., xii, 18; Thomas, xii, 21. SMITH, Abner, xvii, 5; Ann, viii, 23; Benjamin F., iii, 15; Betsey F., xvi, 11; Daniel, xiv, 48; Fanny, xvii, 5; Francis P., viii, 24; Grace, iii, 15; James F., xvi, 11; John, iii. 14; Josiah, xvii, 32; Lemuel, xvii, 12; Margaret, xvi, 14; Nancy, xvi, 12; Nathaniel, xvi, 11; xvi, 13; Rapsima G., ii, 16; Samuel, xiv, 37; Susanna, xvii, 13; Thomas, iii, 14; William, xvi, 15; ——, xvi, 11. SOUTHWORTH, Hannah, xiv, 36. SPAULDING, Sally, xix, 44; Stephen H., xix, 44. SPRAGUE, Margaret L., xviii, 26; Mary, xviii, 26; Samuel M., xviii, 26. SQUIRE, Sally, xii, 9. STEVENS, James, v, 2; Maryan, v, 4; William, v, 3. STONE, Daniel, xvi, 1. STOW, Betsey, xviii, 36; Edward, xviii, 33; George, xix, 36; Lydia F., xviii, 31; Nathaniel, xi, 21; Timothy, xviii, 32. STOWELL, Hannah, xvii, 21; Joel, xvii, 1; Sarah, xvii, 2. STRONG, Ann E., xv, 2; William F., xi, 2; William I., xi, 1. SUMNER, Alice, xv, 18; Eliza, xv, 18; Seth, xv, 18. SWAN, Joseph, xvi, 32; Joseph W., xvi, 32; Nancy, xvi, 32; Robert, x, 6. SWEET, Elizabeth, xviii, 3.

TALBOT, Ann S., xix, 14; George, xix, 14; George G., xix, 14; Josiah, xvii, 23; Lucy, xvii, 22; Martha, xvii, 19; Nathaniel, xvii, 20; Sylvester W, xix, 14; xix, 14. THOMPSON, Catherine, vi, 6; Norman, vi, 6; Sibel, xvii, 11. THORNTON, Augustus T., xviii, 14; Jane A., xviii, 15; Joseph, xviii, 14. TOWNSEND, Jonathan, xix, 42. TRASK, Luke, xvii, 16. TURNER, Amelia L., xiv, 28; Danford, xv, 8; Ebenezer, xv, 8; Francis E., xiv, 28; James, xv, 8; Jemima, xv, 8; Joel, xv, 8; Lavina R., xiv, 28; Sally, xv, 8. TYLER, Eunice, xix, 53.

UPHAM, J. Virgil, xiii, 6. UPTON, Theodore J., xi, 8.

WALLEY, James H., xiii, 5. WEATHERBEE, Comfort, xvi, 16; Rene, xvi, 16; Submit, xi, 29. WELCH, Joel, xviii, 5. WENTWORTH, Bethiah, xix, 22; Jason, xix, 22. WHITE, Eben, xii, 9; George, xii, 9; Luther, xii, 9; xii, 9; Rebecca J., xii, 9. WHITEEN, Aaron, iii, 11. WHITING, Abigail, v, 12; Abner, xi, 18; Catharine, vi, 22; Elizabeth, v, 10; v, 11; vi, 23; vii, 18; viii, 20; Elizabeth P., xi, 19; Esther, iii, 1; Fisher, v, 13; Francis, vi, 24; Isaac, vi, 16; ix, 11; ix, 12; James, xiii, 38; Joe, xvi, 38; Jonathan, xi, 7; Joseph, ii, 14; Joshua, vii, 15; xi, 19; Locada, xi, 17; Lydia, xvi, 35; Mary, ii, 15; xi, 19; xi, 19; Nathaniel, v, 9; Polly, ii, 13; Rebecca, vi, 16; ix, 9; Ruth, ix, 14; Samuel, iii, 16; xii, 1; xii, 2; Sarah, ix, 10; Solomon, viii, 3; Timothy, viii, 4; xvi, 7; William, xvi, 37. WHITNEY, Samuel S., xix, 44; Sarah W., xix, 44; Stillman S., xix, 44. WIGHT, Joseph, xiii, 12; xix, 4; Mary, xix, 5; Sarah, xiii, 11. WILLIAMS, Ebenezer, v, 15. WILSON, Abigail, xix, 34; Anna, xix, 29; Ebenezer, xix, 29; Ephraim, xvii, 35; xix, 27; Esther, xix, 34; Hannah, xvii, 36; John, xix, 28; xix, 34; xix, 34; John F., xix, 34; Lydia, xix, 32; Maria O., xix, 34; Molly, xix, 34; Polly L., xix, 34. WOODCOCK, John, xviii, 20; Sarah, xviii, 19. WOODS, Caroline A., xvii, 15; Emmeline M., xv, 17; Mary A., xvii, 15; Mary I., xvii, 15; William G., xvii, 15.

EPITAPHS.

—— RANGE I. ——

COBB. i, 1. Jonathan Holmes Cobb. Born July 8, 1799. Died March 12, 1882. Register of Probate Court from 1833 to 1870. Town Clerk from 1845 to 1875. Sophia Doggett, wife of Jonathan H. Cobb, born May 23, 1805, died January 13, 1878, aged 72 years, 7 months, and 21 days.

FAIRBANKS. i, 2. In memory of Mr. Ebenezer Fairbanks, who died Nov. 21, 1832. Aet. 75.

Friends nor physicians could not save, Nor can the grave confine it here,
This mortal body from the grave; When Christ doth call it to appear.

FAIRBANKS. i, 3. In memory of Mary, wife of Ebenezer Fairbanks, who died Jan. 7, 1843. Aet. 87. Erected by her children.

> Though thou hast left us, mother, each kind deed,
> And word, and thought of thine, shall with us live,
> And though our hearts at thy departure bleed,
> These to our souls a bright example give:
> Like the ripe sheaf, when harvest time has come,
> Mature in goodness, God has brought thee home.

FAIRBANKS. i, 4. Prudence Fairbanks died Mar. 20, 1871, aged 89 years.

FAIRBANKS. i, 5. In memory of Mrs. Prudence Fairbank, wife of Mr. Ebenezer Fairbank, who died Nov. 11th, 1815, aged 78.

GAY. i, 6. Sacred to the memory of Miss Mary Gay, who died April 29th, 1813. Aged 81.

MESSENGER. i, 7. In memory of Mrs. Olive, wife of Mr. Jason Messenger, who died Nov. 5, 1837. Aet. 57.

> Her spirit is with God, and this its plea:
> My Savior lives, my Savior died for me.

MESSENGER. i, 8. In memory of Henry, son of Mr. Jason and Mrs. Olive Messenger, who died Oct. 8, 1827, Aet. 17 yrs. and 6 mo.

> Smitten friends are angels sent on errands full of love;
> For us they languish and for us they die:
> And shall they languish, shall they die in vain?

NICHOLSON. i, 9. Maria Nicholson died Jan. 10, 1850, aged 65 years.
Elizabeth R. Nicholson, born March 10, 1800, died June 1, 1878.
Daughters of Commodore Samuel Nicholson, United States Navy.

DEDHAM CEMETERY EPITAPHS.

—— RANGE II. ——

ARBONNE. ii, 1. In memory of Charlotte Arbonne, (only daugh' of Mr. Anthony Arbonne, merc' of Boston, dec'd) who died May 13, 1809. Aet. 23.

> My mother dear, do not lament, but know
> God orders thee to stay and me to go.
> Now learn with patience meekly to submit
> To whatsoe'er God's wisdom judges best,
> To say with humble Job, the Lord thinks fit:
> Giving or taking, let his Name be blest.

FAIRBANKS. ii, 2. In memory of Mr. Eben' Fairbanks, who died Feb. 12th, 1812. Aged 79 years.

DEWIN. ii, 3. Sacred to the memory of Mrs. Margaret Dewin, who died Dec' 12th, 1811. Aged 84.

GAY. ii, 4. In memory of Mr. Josiah Gay who died Sep. 14, 1804. Aet. 84.

GAY. ii, 5. In memory of Mr. Moses Gay who died May 23d, 1804. Aet. 64.

GAY. ii, 6. Sacred to the memory of Mrs. Sarah Gay, Relict of Mr. Ebenezer Gay, who died Feb. 21, 1843. Aet. 89 years.

GAY. ii, 7. Sacred to the memory of Mr. Ebenezer Gay, who died Feb. 23, 1824. Aet. 78.

GAY. ii, 8. In memory of Mrs. Sarah Gay, wife of Capt. Daniel Gay, who died June 8, 1808. Aet. 04.

GAY. ii, 9. In memory of Capt. Daniel Gay, who died Feb. 24, 1798. Aged 84 years.

GAY. ii, 10. In memory of Mr. Daniel Gay, who died 15 April, A. D. 1801. Aged 63 years.

MESSENGER. ii, 11. John, son of Mr. Jason and Mrs. Olive Messenger, died July 25, 1812. Aet.-5.

> While with the spirits of the just
> My Savior I adore.
> I smile upon my sleeping dust,
> That now can weep no more.

MESSENGER. ii, 12. Newton, son of Mr. Jason and Mrs. Olive Messenger, died Feb. 8th, 1805. Aged 4 months.

> Stop daring Cavilist! t'is God who calls
> His favorites from the sick'ning ills of life.
> His hand but lightly on the infant falls,
> And cuts it off from sorrow, toil and strife.

WHITING. ii, 13. Polly Whiting, daur. of Mr. Hezekiah and Mrs. Mary Whiting, died Sept. 22d, 1706. Aged 2 yrs. and 24 days.

WHITING. ii, 14. In memory of Dea. Joseph Whiting, who died Nov. 10th, 1806. Aged 77 years.

The hoary head is a crown of glory, if it be found in the way of righteousness. Blessed are the dead who die in the Lord. The corruptible must put on incorruption, and this mortal must put on immortality.

WHITING. ii, 15. In memory of Mrs. Mary, the wife of Dea. Joseph Whiting, who died April 10th, 1811. Aet. 83.

The days of our years are three score years and ten, and if by reason of strength they be fourscore years, yet is their strength labor and sorrow, for it is soon cut off, and we fly away.

SMITH. ii, 16. In memory of Mrs. Rapsima G. wife of Mr. Whiting Smith, who died March 4, 1840. Aet. 20. Here reposeth beneath this sacred stone, the affectionate wife and Mother, the loving Daughter and Friend.

FALES. ii, 17. Nathaniel Fales died Sept. 26, 1854. Aet. 74 yrs. 6 mos.
Blessed are the dead who die in the Lord.
Rebecca, wife of Nath¹ Fales, died Sept. 7, 1862. Aet. 81 yrs. 4 mos.

LEWIS. ii, 18. Sacred to the memory of Mr. Paul Lewis, who died Jan. 30, 1834. Aet. 74.

LEWIS. ii, 19, In memory of Mrs. Eunice Lewis, wife of Mr. Paul Lewis, died May 10, 1828. Aet. 67 yrs. A friend in need, a friend in deed—to all in distress lies here at quiet rest.

LEWIS. ii, 20. In memory of Mr. Asa Lewis, son of Mr. Paul and Mrs. Eunice Lewis, who died Jan'y 23, 1808, in his 25th year.

I've paid the debt that all must pay,   Tho' cruel Death has conquered me
Tho awful to my view;   The victory is but small,
On frightful rocks where waters poured, For I shall rise and live again,
And broken buildings flew.   And Death himself shall fall.

LEWIS. ii, 21. In memory of Capt. Samuel Lewis who died July 23, 1854, aged 66 years.
Anna, wife of Capt. Samuel Lewis died Aug. 9, 1869. Aet. 77 years.

HAPGOOD. ii, 22. Catherine A. died Oct. 27, 1834. Aet. 17. Henry M. Nov. —, 1844. Aet. 30. Lucy Ann, Dec. 5, 1845. Aet. 26. Adeline R., Dec. 9, 1846. Aet. 34. Catherine Conant died Apr. 5, 1850. Aet. 73. Wife and children of Henry Hapgood.
Henry Hapgood died Oct. 29, 1861. Aet. 74.

DOWSE, SHAW. ii, 23. (South side.) In memory of Edward Dowse, Sarah Dowse, Samuel Shaw, and Hannah Shaw.

(East side.) Here rest the Remains of Edward Dowse, A Representative of this District in the Congress of the United States. His Philanthropy was universal, His Benevolence active and unostentatious. By assiduous and learned Research his Faith was established in the Gospel of Christ, and his life was a bright example of its power. He died on the 3ᵈ of September, 1828, in the 72 year of his age.

(West side.) Samuel Shaw was born in Boston on the 2ᵈ of September 1754. He served his country as an officer in the American Army during the war of the Revolution. After the Peace of 1783, being the first Consul of the United States in China, he had a leading influence in establishing important Commercial relations between these nations. A Soldier without Fear: A Merchant without Reproach: he combined a chivalric spirit with a highly cultivated Mind. He died at sea and was buried in the Indian Ocean on the 30th of May, 1793.

(North side.) Sarah Dowse, the widow of Edward Dowse, died on the 3ᵈ of July, 1839, aged 83. Hannah Shaw, the widow of Samuel Shaw, died on the 24th of January, 1833, aged 77. They were Twin Sisters, and daughters of William Phillips of Boston. Pious and charitable, they were united through life by Nature, Fortune and Affection, and they here rest together.

[*Note.*—Near the Dowse monument is a nameless tomb which contains the bodies of Josiah Smith and his son Thomas, and probably other members of their families.]

—— RANGE III. ——

WHITING. iii, 1. In memory of Mrs. Esther Whiting, the wife of Mr. Stephen Whiting, died Dec. 23^d, 1790, aged 57 years.

It was, I lived, but now my day   My spirit's gone: it lives; but where,
To dust is mouldering fast away   Ask not; Repent; for death prepare.

BAKER. iii, 2. In memory of the widow Elizabeth Baker who died 4th Feb. 1803, aged 95 years.

FAIRBANKS. iii, 3. Sacred to the memory of Jason Fairbanks, who departed this life 10th Sept. 1801. Aged 21 years.

FAIRBANKS. iii, 4. In memory of Mr. Calvin Fairbanks who died 23 Nov. 1800. Aet. 22 years.

Depart my friends wipe off all tears,   Here I must lye till Christ appears.

BATES. iii, 5. In memory of Mr. Samuel Bates who died 21 Aug. 1800, aged 43 years.

GUILD. iii, 6. In memory of Mrs. Miriam, wife of Joseph Guild, Esq. who died Sept. 27, 1831. Aet. 93.

GUILD. iii, 7. In memory of Joseph Guild, Esq. who died Dec. 28th 1794, aged 60 years.

Draw near, my friends, and think on me,   Now I lie mouldering in the dust,
I once was in this world like thee;   In hope to rise among the just.

GUILD. iii, 8. In memory of Mrs. Catherine Guild, the wife of Mr. Reuben Guild, who died Sept. 8th 1795, aged 25 years.

In youth I've walked the way to death,   By me, my mates, a warning take,
Obey'd my God who gave me breath;   Prepare for death before's too late.

MASON. iii, 9. In memory of Abigail Mason, the wife of Mr. Thaddeus Mason, who departed this life July 29th 1796, aged 28 years.

She died in Jesus and is bless'd,
How soft her slumbers are!
From sufferings and from sins released,
And free from ev'ry snare.

FULLER. iii, 10. In memory of Miss Judith Fuller, died Feb. 8th 1815. Aged 82 years.

WHITEEN. iii, 11. In memory of Mr. Aaron Whiteen, who died Octr 18th, 1792. Aged 42 years, 7 months, and 12 days.

HUMPHREY. iii, 12. In memory of Mrs. Sarah Humphrey, the wife of Jonas Humphrey, who died Feb. 24th 1794. Aged 65 years.

FALIES. iii, 13. In memory of Capt. David Falies, who died Jan 23^d 1793. Aet. 91.

FIRST PARISH. 17

Also Mrs. Mary Falies, the wife of Capt. David Falies, who died Dec. 24th 1793, Aet. 78.

SMITH. iii, 14. To the memory of Mr. John Smith, a native of England, who died 27 Jan. 1801, aged 43 years.

Also Thomas Smith, son of Mr. John and Mrs. Grace Smith, died 1 Feb. 1799, aged four years.

> Reader seek not his merits to disclose,
> Or draw his frailties from their dread abode,
> There they alike in trembling hope repose,
> The bosom of his father and his God.

SMITH. iii, 15. In memory of Mrs. Grace Smith, (widow of Mr. John Smith, both natives of England,) who died Nov. 20, 1825. Æ. 60. And also of Benjamin Franklin Smith, (their son) who died Oct. 17, 1812. Æ. 16.

WHITING. iii, 16. In memory of Mr. Samuel Whiting, who died Jan. 18th, 1808, in the 81 year of his age.

———RANGE IV.———

KEITH. iv, 1. In memory of Miss Chloe Keith of Dudley, Daugh'r of Capt. David and Mrs. Ruth Keith. Died June 17th 1780 in ye 14th year of her age. (Headstone removed since 1869, but the footstone still remains.)

LUCE. iv. 2. Charley A. Luce died May 3d 1876. Age 1 year 6 m. 9 d.

FAIRBANKS. iv, 3. Calvin, only son of Joshua and Clarissa Fairbanks, died Feb. 13, 1837, Aet. 12 years,

> Behold and see as you pass by,   As I am now, so you must be.
> As you are now, so once was I.   Prepare for death and follow me.

FAIRBANKS. iv, 4. In memory of Calvin Fairbanks, son of Mr. Joshua and Mrs. Clarissa Fairbanks, who died Sept. 18th 1820. Aged 1 year and 1 month.

> No more the smiling babe is seen,
> Behold the gaping tomb!
> The tender plant so fresh and green
> Has met its final doom.

DRAPER. iv, 5. In memory of Mrs. Lydia Draper, wife of Mr. William Draper, who died Jan. 25, 1790: in the 34th year of her age.

> Time was like you I life possest
> And Time shall be when you must rest.

MASON. iv, 6. Mason. Abigail obt. July 29, 1796 Aet. 28. Anne, obt. June 26, 1828 Aet. 58. Thaddeus, obt. Feb. 13, 1832, aet. 70. John obt. May 18, 1836 aet. 26. Thaddeus Harris, obt. in Memphis, Tenn. Dec. 11, 1843. Aet. 36.

FARRINGTON. iv, 7. In memory of Mrs. Hannah Farrington, wife of Ebenezer Farrington, who died July 21, 1788, Aet. 52.

FARRINGTON. iv. 8. In memory of Mr. Abner Farrington, son of Mr. Ebenezer and Mrs. Hannah Farrington, who died Nov. 14, 1789. Aet. 34.

FARRINGTON. iv. 9, Sacred to the memory of Mr. Ebenezer Farrington. who departed this life Oct. 25th 1810, in his 76th year.

Death is a welcome messenger to the good man.
Though here his mouldering body lies,   The wintry storms of life are past,
His spirit dwells above the skies;   And heaven shall be his home at last.

FARRINGTON. iv, 10. Ebenezer Farrington died Apr. 10, 1848, aged 88 years. Elizabeth, his wife, died Feb. 1857 aged 90 years.

FARRINGTON. iv. 11. [Stone broken; this remains]: arrington, who died Sept. 19, 1805. Aet. 43.

———RANGE V.———

NICHOLS. v, 1. In memory of Lieut. Abel Nichols, of Danvers, who died Septr 12th, 1778, in the 36th year of his age.

STEVENS. v, 2. In memory of James Stevens who died Decr 20th 1786, in the 33^d year of his age.

STEVENS. v, 3. In memory of Mr. William Stevens who died Octr 5, 1777, in the 77th year of his age.

He was a good citizen, and an honest man.

STEVENS. v, 4. In memory of the Widow Maryan Stevens who died June 21st 1794 in the 84th year of her age.

Blessed are the Dead that die in the Lord.

FARRINGTON. v, 5. In memory Miss Mehitable Farrington who died Nov. 4th 1803 aged 22 years.

DRAPER. v, 6. In memory of Ebenezer Draper, son of Mr. William and Mrs. Lydia Draper, died Feby 20, 1788 aged 1 year, 9 months, 14 days.

PARKER. v, 7. Catharine Parker, dau'r of Mr. Jonathan and Mrs. Catharine Parker, died 22^d Sept. 1800 aged 14 months and 27 days.

Her life was short, but pleasant.

The Lord gave and the Lord hath taken away.

PARKER. v, 8. Alexander A. Parker son of Mr. Jonathan and Mrs. Catharine Parker died Dec. 27, 1804. Aged 3 years.

Blessed are the dead that die in the Lord.

WHITING. v, 9. In memory of Mr. Nathl Whiting, died Sept. 2, 1821. Aged 69 years.

WHITING. v, 10. In memory of Mrs. Elizabeth, wife of Nathaniel Whiting who died Nov. 15, 1841. Aet. 86.

WHITING. v, 11. In memory of Miss Elizabeth Whiting, Daugh. of Mr. Nathl and Mrs. Elizth Whiting, died Nov. 10, 1817, aged 25 yrs.

WHITING. v, 12. Abigail Whiting died Oct. 7, 1867. Aet. 73.

WHITING. v, 13. In memory of Mr. Fisher Whiting who died March 25th 1797, aged 40 years.

RICHARDS. v. 14. Sally Richards, dau^r of Mr. Reuben and Mrs. Sarah Richards, died Nov. 5th, 1795, aged 5 years.

WILLIAMS. v, 15. Here lies the body of Mr. Ebenezer Williams, Preacher of the gospel (son to Col^l Eben^r Williams of Pomfret and Jerusha his wife) who died May ye 28, 1777, in ye 23^d year of his age.

Blessed are the dead that die in the Lord.

FIRST PARISH.

FISHER. v, 16. In memory of Miss Rebecca Fisher who died 29 July, 1797, in the 24 year of her age.

Here when fleeting life is ended Look beyond these narrow graves,
Vain distinctions all are blended, Saints are kings, and sinners slaves.

EATON, BALCH. v, 17. Calvin Eaton, obt. Aug. 31, 1809; aged 31. Isaac Eaton, obt. Jan. 16, 1822; aged 75. Isaac Eaton, jr. obt. Sept. 13, 1838, aged 62. Sarah Eaton obt. Feb. 10, 1844, aged 95.

Rev. William Balch, obt. Aug. 31, 1842, aged 67 years.

——RANGE VI.——

GUILD. vi, 1. In memory of Nath¹, son of Mr. John and Mrs. Rebecca Guild, who died Sept. 23, 1805, aged 1 year.

GUILD, EATON. vi, 2. Nath¹ Guild Died Sept. 23, 1805. Aet. 1 year. Alfred R. Guild, died in Galveston, Texas, Sept. 3, 1837. Aet. 30. Miranda Guild died Mar. 20, 1873. Aet. 74. John Guild Died Dec. 2, 1847. Aet. 75. Rebecca Eaton. wife of John Guild, died Sept. 7, 1849. Aet. 77. Capt. John Eaton died May 14, 1777. Aet. 45. Mrs. Desire Eaton, his wife, died Aug. 3, 1814. Aet. 83.

CURRIEA. vi, 3. Caroline S. Curriea, born Sept. 6, 1822, died Nov. 7, 1883. Ever thoughtful of the comfort of others, a loving mother and faithful friend.

PAUL. vi, 4. In memory of Mr. William Paul, who died Dec. 10, 1791. Aet. 63 years. Also Mrs. Mary Paul, wife of Mr. William Paul, died Nov. 18ᵗʰ 1791. Aet. 59 years.

Come living friends see where we lie, But to prepare for death and He'v'n.
Remember you are born to die: Is all for which the longest life is given.

CAIN. vi, 5. John P. Cain died December 9, 1827, aged 37 years. John E. M. Cain, son of John P. and Elizabeth Cain, died July 8, 1847, aged 26 years. Mrs. Elizabeth Cain died Mar. 19, 1857, aged 72 years.

I know that my Redeemer liveth.

THOMPSON. vi, 6. In memory of Mrs. Catherine Thompson, a native of Chester, Nova Scotia, who died at Needham, Feb. 1, 1855. Aet. 23.

In the same grave rests her son Norman, who died at Boston Feb. 24, 1840.

There is rest in heaven.

LEWIS. vi, 7. In memʳ of Mrs. Abigail Lewis, (wife of Mr. John Lewis,) She died May yᵉ 6ᵗʰ 1777. Aged 60 years.

LEWIS. vi, 8. Near this place are deposited the remains of Mr. Joseph Lewis, who died June 9, 1804, aged 66 years.

> Here lies entombed beneath this mossy sod
> An honest man, "the noblest work of God,"
> In whom those beauties of a noble mind,
> Faith and good works were happily combined:
> A friend and comfort to the sick and poor,
> Want never knocked unheeded at his door:
> A tender husband, father, brother, friend,
> He crowned his virtues with a pious end.

LEWIS. vi, 9. To the memory of Mrs. Molly Lewis, relict of the late Mr. Joseph Lewis, who died Oct. 2, 1816, aged 75 years.

In life how peaceful moved this happy pair,
How blessed in death released from mortal care.
Ye angels o'er their dust your vigils keep.
Calm be their slumbers undisturbed their sleep.
And ye who tread in solemn silence near
Repress the sigh, restrain the swelling tear.
No more to wound, shall earthly sorrows fly,
Eternal bliss awaits them in the sky.

LEWIS. vi, 10. Sacred to the memory of Miss Sally Lewis, dau. of Mr. Joseph and Mrs. Sally Lewis, who departed this life 13 July, 1797, aged 16 years.

Nature with copious grief laments the dead,
A mothers tears bedew the verdant sod!
On outstretch'd wings her cherished hopes are fled,
But sorrow points to a Redeeming God.

HAMMER. vi, 11. Wm P. Hammer died Jan. 18th 1887, aged four years and three months.

LIEBOLD. vi, 12. Our Father, George J. Liebold died Feb. 20, 1880, aged 49 years 1 month 6 days.

LIEBOLD. vi, 13. Our Mother, Caroline Liebold died June 5, 1882, aged 40 years, 10 months, 27 days.

MASON. vi, 14. In memory of Miss Rhoda Mason, Daug^r of Mr. William and Mrs. Hannah Mason, who died Feby 1st, 1781, in the 21st year of her age.

Cheerful I go at Jesus call   Come welcome Death she meekly cry'd
To be with Christ is best of all: Breathed out her patient soul and dy'd.

RICHARDS. vi, 15. Samuel Richards born Mar. 16, 1756, died Dec. 22, 1822. Phebe Willard, wife of Samuel Richards, born April 8, 1758, died June 8, 1782. Olive Mason, wife of Samuel Richards, born Dec. 21, 1758, died Jany. 20, 1837.

Children of Samuel and Olive Richards:

Hannah Richards, born Sept. 1, 1785, died July 12, 1807. Roxana Richards, born Apr. 16, 1796, died Jan. 15, 1813. Seth Richards, born June 10, 1798, died June 2, 1819. Betsey Richards, born Sept. 2, 1794, died Oct. 12, 1821. Danford Richards, born May 4, 1803, died Mar. 17, 1847. Mason Richards, born May 28, 1789, died Feb. 14, 1806. Eliza Richards, born Oct. 7. 1790, died Feb. 18, 1880.

Roxana L. Richards, daughter of Mason and Eliza Richards, born Dec. 6, 1814, died Sept. 18, 1876.

WHITING. vi, 16. In memory of Mr. Isaac Whiting who died July ye 18th, 1785. Ae. 63.. In memory of Mrs. Rebecca Whiting, relict of Mr. Isaac Whiting, who died April ye 13th, 1787. Ae. 65.

DEXTER. vi, 17. [A tomb, over which is a marble slab containing the following texts of Scripture:] This corruptible must put on incorruption.—1 Cor. xv, 53. Our Savior, Jesus Christ, hath abolished death and brought life and immortality to light.—2 Tim. 1: 10. I am the resurrection and the life; he that believeth in me, though he were dead, yet shall he live.—John xi: 25. Behold He is coming in the clouds, and every eye shall see Him.—Rev. i: 7. When Christ our life shall appear, then shall ye also appear with Him in glory.— Col. iii: 4. Where is thy sting, O Death? Where is thy victory, O Grave? Thanks to God, who giveth us the victory through our Lord Jesus Christ.—1 Cor. xv: 55, 57.

FIRST PARISH.

FISHER. vi, 18. In memory of Mr. Josiah Fisher, who died Dec. 19, 1812. Aet. 67.
> With patience to the last he did submit.
> And murmur'd not at what the Lord tho't fit.
> He with a Christian courage did resign,
> His soul to God at his appointed time.

FISHER, vi, 19. In memory of Mr. Josiah Fisher Junr who died Aug. 10, 1794, in the 23^d year of his age.
> My dear young friends come near and see
> A friend of yours I used to be.
> O make your peace with God above,
> The fountain of Eternal love.

PAUL. vi, 20. In memory of Mr. Ebenezer Paul, who died Octr 2, 1804, in the 22^d year of his age.

PAUL. vi, 21. Samuel Paul died March 1, 1775. Aet. 87. Abigail, wife of Samuel Paul, died Sept. 19, 1781. Aet. 83. Ebenezer Paul, died Aug. 20, 1803. Aet. 65. Abigail, wife of Ebenezer Paul, died Jan. 5, 1804. Aet. 55. Isaac Paul, died April 4, 1852. Aet. 77. Lydia, wife of Isaac Paul, died May 5, 1854. Aet. 75.

WHITING. vi, 22. Catharine, Daughter of Calvin and Elizabeth Whiting, died July 5, 1811. Ae. 15 years.

WHITING. vi, 23. In Memory of Mrs. Elizabeth Whiting, wife of Col. Eaton Whiting, who died Jan. 10, 1821. Aet. 27.

WHITING. vi, 24. Francis, son of Eaton and Olive Whiting, died Nov. 4, 1834. Aged 12 days.

——RANGE VII.——

BAKER. vii, 1. Eliphalet Baker died Nov. 9, 1841. Aet. 76. Anne Eaton, wife of Eliphalet Baker, died Oct.! 30, 1853. Aet. 84. Nathaniel Baker, died July 11, 1800. Aet. 17 mo. Nathaniel Baker, died Nov. 19, 1802. Aet. 15 mo. Children of Eliphalet and Anne Baker.

FESSENDEN. vii, 2. John Fessenden, born March 13, 1794, died May 11, 1871. Nancy B. Fessenden, his wife, born Oct. 3, 1803, died May 18, 1886. George Fessenden, born July 9, 1833, died Nov. 20, 1856.

EATON. vii, 3. In memory of Capt. John Eaton who died May 14, 1777. Aged 46 years.

EATON. vii, 4. In memory of Mrs. Desire Eaton, ;wife of Capt. John Eaton, who died August 3^d, 1814. Aged 83 years.

BAKER, vii, 5. John Baker, sheriff of the county of Norfolk, died Jany. 1, 1843. Aged 63 years. Patty Ellis, wife of John Baker, born Nov. 11, 1790, Died Feb. 14, 1876.

PIERSON. vii, 6. The Rev. Jacob Pierson died in Boston, Aug. 12, 1850. Aet. 66. A presbyter of the Protestant Episcopal Church. This memorial is erected by his clerical brethren.

KINGSBURY. vii, 7. In memory of Mrs. Mary Kingsbury, who departed this life Aug. 24, 1788. Aged 85 years.
> In faith she lived, in dust she lies,
> But Faith fore sees the dust shall rise.

KINGSBURY. vii, 8. Here lie the remains of Mr. Joseph Kingsbury. He departed this life Aug. y° 17th 1775, in y° 56 year of his Age.

> Death is a debt to Nature due,
> As I have paid it, so must you.

DAY. vii, 9. In memory of Mrs. Prudence Day, widow of the late Maj^r Jonathan Day, who died Sept. 4th 1807. Aet. 74.

> The sweet remembrance of the just
> Shall flourish while they sleep in dust.

KINGSBURY. vii, 10. George Kingsbury died Augt 14th 1775 in y° 3^d year of his age. Sarah Kingsbury died Augt 14, 1775 in y° 5 year of her age.

> Children of Mr. Joseph and Mrs. Phebe Kingsbury.

BATTLE. vii, 11. Here sleeps in peace the remains of Col. Ebenezer Battle, who made his exit Novr y° 6th, 1776, in y° 46th year of his age.

> When Death invades we must obey,
> Resigne our breath and sleep in clay:
> The Trump shall sound, all must attend,
> Make Heaven your aim and Christ your friend.

BAKER. vii, 12. In memory of Mrs. Chloe Baker, the wife of Mr. Nathaniel Baker, who died Dec. 3^d 1773 in y° 23^d year of her age.

> Behold and see as you pass by   As I am now, so you must be,
> As you be now so once was I.   Prepare for death and follow me.

PAUL. vii, 13. Samuel Paul died July 8, 1833 aged 49 yrs. Martha, wife of Samuel Paul, died Nov. 1, 1857, aged 67 years. Abby P. wife of Samuel Davis, Died Nov. 30, 1846, aged 29 years. Susan F. Paul died Oct. 12, 1862, aged 1 year 4 months.

DRAPER. vii, 14. Here lie interred the Remains of Major Abijah Draper, who departed this life the first day of May, A. D. 1780 aged 45 years.

> Ah! why so soon from us he's fled
> Laments the widow, orphan, friend;
> You must not say, too soon he's dead
> Who stayed to answer life's great end.

WHITING. vii, 15. In memory of Mr. Joshua Whiting who died Oct. y° 3^d 1780, in y° 51st year of his age.

POND. vii, 16. Nathaniel D. Pond, died April 29, 1861. Aet. 35 yrs 7 mos, Flora Maria, wife of N. D. Pond died Oct. 27, 1860. Aet. 40 yrs 2 mos. Charles Davis, son of N. D. & F. M. Pond, died Jan. 24, 1858. Aet. 3 mos. 8 days. Mary Elizabeth, Daughter of N. D. & F. M. Pond, Died May 8, 1868, Aet. 15 years.

POND. vii, 17. Eliph^t Pond, died Jan. 19, 1795. Aet. 91. Elizabeth Pond died Oct. 25, 1789. Aet. 81. Eliph^t Pond Died July 2, 1813. Aet. 68. Prudence Pond died May 18, 1818. Aet. 58. Eliph^t Pond died April 25, 1820. Aet. 35. Henry E. son of Eliph^t and Ann Pond died June 25, 1822. Aet. 2 years. William A. their son; died Aug. 8, 1835. Aet. 8 years. Julia A., Daughter of Eliph^t and Ann Pond, died Nov. 20. 1868. Aet. 47 yrs.

> There is rest in Heaven.

WHITING. vii, 18. In memory of Mrs. Elizabeth Whiting, the wife of Mr. Edward Whiting, who died 8 April, 1798, Aet. 29 ye.

BAKER. vii, 19. Mary, wife of Daniel Baker, died March 15, 1836. Aet. 81.

BAKER. vii. 20. This humble stone is erected to the memory of Mr. Daniel Baker who was removed from this state of trial and suffering May 7th 1806, in the 54 year of his age.

KELTON. vii, 21. This monument is erected to perpetuate the remembrance of Miss Catherine A. Kelton, who died Oct. 20, A. D. 1816, aged 17 years.

Her amiable disposition and the gentleness of her manners, with the unblamable tenor of her life, though short, yet virtuous, and entirely devoted to the happiness of her friends, rendered her dear to the affections of all by whom she was known. Beloved in life—in death lamented,

Tender friends awhile may mourn Dearer, better friends I have,
Me from their embraces torn: In the realms beyond the grave.

---RANGE VIII.---

FAULKNER. viii, 1. Mrs. Elizabeth Whiting Faulkner, Daughter of James and Lucy Morse, died April 17, 1874. Aged 52 years.

The weary soul is at rest in the arms of her Savior in whom her
faith never wavered.

ROBERTS. viii, 2. In memory of Mrs. Nancy, wife of Mr. Edward Roberts, and dau' of Solomon and Lucy Whiting, who died Oct. 24, 1826. Aged 44.

Accept, blest shade,
This last sad tribute of surviving love. E. R.

WHITING. viii, 3. In memory of Mr. Solomon Whiting who died Novr. 5, 1803. Aged 48 years.

WHITING. viii, 4. In memory of Mr. Timothy Whiting who died Jan. 7, 1828, aged 82 years.

Blessed are the merciful for they shall find mercy.

MORSE. viii, 5. In memory of Harriet, daughter of James and Lucy Morse, who died June 17, 1841, aged 17 years.

She being dead yet speaketh.

What say the happy dead? Till life's uneasy dream
She bids us bear our load; In rapture shall depart.
With silent steps proceed She bids us give, like her,
And follow her to God: To Christ our Bleeding Hearts.

MORSE. viii, 6. In memory of Nancy Whiting, daughter of James and Lucy Morse, who died July 22, 1841. Aged 21 years.

Oh! may the mantle of her heavenly deeds
Of faith and love and patience fall on us;
Then naught will hide those mansions
From our view, from which, with loving eye,
She now surveys her kindred here below.

MORSE. viii, 7. James Morse died Jan. 14, 1855; aged 71 years, 10 mos. and 28 days.

MORSE. viii, 8. Lucy, wife of James Morse, died Sept. 2, 1855: aged 70 years, 9 mo. & 20 days.

EATON—ALDEN—BROWNE. viii, 9. John, only child of John and Hannah Eaton, died Sept. 15. 1796, aged 4 years. Lucy wife of John Eaton, jr, died May 13, 1827, aged 25. John Eaton died March 24, 1842, aged 78. Hannah, widow of John Eaton, died June 3, 1860, aged 98 ys. 7 mo. Lucy Eaton died Oct. 7, 1800, aged 4 yrs. 4 mos. John Ellis Eaton died Oct. 23, 1800, aged 2 years 8 months. Children of Luther & Lucy Eaton.

Capt. Luther Eaton died Nov. 13, 1820, aged 54. Eliza, wife of Luther Eaton, died Sept. 28, 1844, aged 42. Lucy, widow of Capt. Luther Eaton, died Feb. 15, 1847, aged 75 years. J. Ellis Eaton died Oct. 7, 1854, aged 20. Maria Eaton died Dec. 20, 1863, aged 63. Abby M. Daur. of J. and A. Eaton died Feb. 26, 1848, Aet. 8 mos. Luther Eaton died May 17th 1876, aged 73 years, 10 days. Joel Eaton died Nov. 25, 1881, aged 75 years, 10 mos. 4 days. Abigail, wife of Joel Eaton, died May 14, 1883, aged 72 yrs. 10 mos. 19 days.

George Alden died Aug. 25, 1862: Aet. 58 years. Hannah, widow of George Alden, died Mar, 6, 1878, Aet. 74 years. Martha, wife of Horace E. Browne, died Feb. 24, 1876. Aet. 44 years.

FALES. viii, 10. Charles S. son of William & Mary J. Fales died Sept. 11, 1827 aged 2 yrs. 8 mos.

FALES. viii, 11. Mary L. Fales, born Sept. 13, 1793, died July 22, 1882.
Stephen Fales, born Dec. 5, 1786, died Dec. 3, 1860.

REDIHOUGH. viii, 12. James W. died Aug. 5, 1879, in the 19th year of his age. Elizabeth A. died Feb. 14, 1876, aged 9 years, 6 mos.
Children of Thomas and Ellen Redihough.

> We have entered the valley of blessing so sweet
> And Jesus abides with us there;
> And there's rest for the weary-worn traveller's feet,
> And joy for the sorrowing heart.

LEWIS. viii, 13. Margaret A., wife of Levi C. Lewis, died Aug. 7, 1879, aged 75 yrs. Lydia J. dau. Levi C. and Margaret A. Lewis, died June 4, 1860, aged 17 yrs. 3 mos.

LEWIS. viii, 14. Levi C. Lewis died Nov. 19, 1877, aged 72 yrs. 10 mos. Helena M., dau. of Levi C. and Margaret A. Lewis, died July 27, 1872, aged 43 years.

DRAPER. viii, 15. In memory of Capt. James Draper, who died April ye 24th, 1768, in ye 77th year of his age.

In memory of Mrs. Abigail Draper, wife of Capt. James Draper, who died Nov^{ber} ye 23, 1797, in ye 70th year of her age.

2 Sam. i: 23—They were lovely and pleasant in their Lives & in their Death they were not divided.

The stroke of Death hath laid my head   The Trump shall sound: I hope to rise
Down in this dark & Silent Bed;   And meet my Savior in the skies.

DRAPER. viii, 16. Abijah Draper, son of Mr. Ira & Mrs. Lydia Draper, died 4 Oct. 1802, aged 9 mos.

DRAPER. viii, 17. In memory of Mrs. Alice Draper, wife of Maj^r Abijah Draper, who died Jany 22^d, 1777, aged 36 years.

DRAPER. viii, 18. Lucy Chickering Draper, dau. of Mr. Ira & Mrs. Lydia Draper, died 15 Sept. 1800, aged 3 yrs. and 3 mos.

DRAPER. viii, 19. In memory of Mrs. Desire Draper, relict of Maj^r Abijah Draper. Died Oct. 23, 1815. Aet. 69.

She sleeps in Jesus, wipe the falling tear.
She lives in glory, strive to meet her there.

WHITING. viii, 20. In memory of Mrs. Elizabeth, wife of Mr. Joshua Whiting, who Died March 27th, 1770, in ye 41 year of her age.

POND. viii, 21. In memory of Miss Rebecca Pond, Dau^r of Eliphalet Pond, Esq., and Elizabeth his wife. Died April 13th 1776, in the 28 year of her age.

POND. viii, 22. In Memory of Mrs. Elizabeth Pond, wife of Eliphalet Pond, Esq., who died the 25th of Oct. 1789, in the 81st year of her age.

SMITH. viii, 23. In memory of Mrs. Ann, wife of Mr. William Smith, who died June 28, 1835, aged 36 years.

And while our mournful thoughts deplore
The mother gone, removed the friend
With heart resigned his grace adore,
On whom our nobler hopes depend.

SMITH. viii, 24. Francis Prentice, son of William & Ann Smith, died July 3^d, 1835. Aged 4 years.

Suffer little children to come unto me, and forbid them not, for of such is the kingdom of heaven.

POND. viii, 25. William Allen, son of Eliphalet and Ann Pond, died Aug. 8, 1835. Aet. 8 years.

He's gone to join the happy throng   Then why should we his loss deplore,
Of youthful cherubs round the Throne;   Since he now lives to die no more.

——RANGE IX.——

GAY. ix, 1. Here lies interred the body of Mrs Lydia Gay, only Dau^r to Mr Benjamin and Mrs Hannah Gay, who died Nov. 10, 1756. Aged 25 years & 28 D^s.

AVERY. ix, 2. Here lies buried ye body of Capt. William Avery, who Deceased May 13th, 1750, in the 74th year of his Age.

MARSH. ix, 3. John Marsh died in New York Aug. 24, 1827, aged 27 years. Martin Marsh died in Florida, May 29, 1836, aged 32 years. Henry Marsh died Aug. 13, 1836, aged 34 years. Martin Marsh, born Aug. 27, 1844, died Sept. 20, 1845. Martin Metcalf Marsh, born Sept. 15, 1849, died Sept. 14, 1872. Charles Marsh, born Oct. 13, 1853, died Sept. 13, 1878. Martin Marsh, born April 15, 1777, D. July 26, 1865. Elizabeth Metcalf, wife of Martin Marsh, born May 12, 1778, D. Dec. 31, 1808. Francis Marsh, born Oct. 6, 1806. Died May 4, 1879.

ELLIS. ix, 4. Here lies buried the Body of Mr. Samuel Ellis, who died Nov. 2nd, 1755, in ye 57 year of his age.

DEAN. ix, 5. Here lies the body of Mrs. Mary Dean, the wife of Mr. Joshua Dean. Died April 19, 1756, in the 34 year of her age.

ELLIS. ix, 6. Betsey Ellis died July 14, 1855. Aet. 60.

ELLIS. ix, 7. Jesse Ellis, Born April 30, 1765, Died March 30, 1850. George Ellis, Born Feb. 28, 1819, Died Feb. 4, 1847. Lucy Ellis, Born April 12, 1780, Died Dec. 15, 1865.

GAY. ix, 8. In memory of Mary, wife of Mr. Ebenezer Gay, who died Nov. 17, 1777. Aged 27.

WHITING. ix, 9. Rebecca, daughter of Mr. Isaac & Mrs. Rebecca Whiting, died Dec. 10, 1766, in the 22^d year of her age.

WHITING. ix, 10. In memory of Sarah, Daugh^r of Mr. Isaac & Mrs. Rebecca Whiting, died Nov. 28th, 1775, in ye 12th year of her age.

WHITING. ix, 11. In memory of Isaac, son of Mr. Fisher & Mrs. Rebecca Whiting, who died May 9th, 1785, aged 9 months.

WHITING. ix, 12. Isaac, son of Mr. Fisher & Mrs. Rebecca Whiting, died Sept. 13th, 1793, in the 7th year of his age.

DRAPER. ix, 13. In memory of Abijah Draper, son to Mr. Abijah & Mrs. Alice Draper, who died Dec. 16th, 1774, in ye 11th yr. of his age.

WHITING. ix, 14. In memory of Mrs. Ruth Whiting, wife of Mr. Jeremiah Whiting, who died March ye 30th, 1770, aged 74.

GAY. ix, 15. In memory of Mrs. Mary Gay, relict of Mr. Lusher Gay, who died Oct. 7, 1780, in the 90th year of her age.

GAY. ix, 16. In memory of Mr. Lusher Gay, who died Oct. ye 18th, 1769, in the 85th year of his age.

GAY. ix, 17. In memory of Mrs. Sarah Gay, the wife of Mr. Joseph Gay, who died Feb. 10th, 1773, in ye 29th year of her age.

GAY. ix, 18. In memory of Mr. Joseph Gay, who died Feb. 10, 1814, aged 83 years.

GAY. ix, 19. In memory of Phebe, wife of Mr. Joseph Gay, who died April ye 29th, 1782, in ye 42^d year of her age.

DAVIS. ix, 20. In memory of Washington Davis, son of Capt. Nathaniel and Mrs. Prudence Davis, died Nov. 25th, 1788, in the 11th year of his age.

BROWN. ix, 21. In memory of Mrs. Sarah Brown, wife of George Brown, who died March 18, 1827. Aet. 25.

In the midst of life we are in death.

BROWN. ix, 22. William F., son of George & Eliza Ann Brown, died July 4, 1830. Aet. 4 months & 2 days.

Go beauteous soul to bloom above.

BROWN. ix, 23. Eliza Ann, daughter of George & Eliza Ann Brown, died July 1, 1843. Aet. 5 months.

Of such is the kingdom of heaven.

BROWN. ix, 24. Mr. George Brown died Oct. 3, 1840. Aet. 48.

Blessed are the pure in heart, for they shall see God.

BROWN. ix, 25. Eliza Ann, wife of George Brown, died Sept. 22, 1844. Aet. 42.

ABRAHAM. ix, 26. Sacred to the memory of Mrs. Elizabeth Abraham, who departed this life Mch. 22^d, 1807, aged 69 years.

COOPER. ix, 27. In memory of Mrs. Ann Cooper, wife of Mr. Samuel Cooper, who died July 17, 1808. Æ. 28. Also her infant son, Sam., who died Sept. 3, 1808. Ae. 3 M^o.

FIRST PARISH.

—— RANGE X. ——

GAY. x, 1. In memory of Mrs. Elizabeth Gay, widow of Mr. John Fisher & Mr. Ezra Gay, who died Dec. 13th, 1796, aged 78 years.

[*Note.*—This stone has been removed since 1870.]

GAY. x, 2. In memory of Mrs Mary Gay, (widow of Mr John Gay), who died July ye 24, 1773, in ye 70 year of her age.

In memory of Mr. John Gay, who died Mch. ye 24, 1753, in the 69 year of his age.

FULLER. x, 3. Here lies ye body of Mrs. Judith Fuller, wife of Mr. John Fuller. She died Novr 19th, 1718, in the 70th year of her age.

GAY. x, 4. Here lies Buried the Body of Mrs Sarah Gay, wife to Mr. John Gay, Dec^d July ye 5th, 1732, in ye 50 year of her age.

PARKER. x, 5. Mrs. Sarah, wife of Mr. Alpha Parker, died June 13, 1842. Aet. 30.

SWAN. x, 6. Here lies buried the Body of Mr. Robert Swan, who Died Oct. 31st, 1773. Aged 75 years.

ADAMS. x, 7. Sarah Jane, dau. of Charles and Mary Jane Adams, died April 9, 1842. Aged 1 year 18 ds.

ALLWRIGHT. x, 8. Alfred Allwright, born May 13, 1815, died Nov. 14, 1873.

They rest from their labors and their works do follow them.

DOGGETT. x, 9.   Memento Mori.

In memory of Mr. Samuel Doggett, who died March 6th, 1794. Aet. 67.

This grave contains the feeble, mouldering clay:
The spirit triumphs in eternal day.

CLAPP. x, 10. Jesse Clapp, died Jan. 19, 1823, aged 51 years. Betsey Doggett, his wife, died Dec. 20, 1850, aged 72 yrs.

Their Children:

Mary, died Oct. 3, 1800. Aet. 2 yrs. Elizabeth D., died June 24, 1810. Aet. 9 yrs. Mary Ann, died July 15, 1816. Aet. 10 years. John D., died Feb. 11, 1878. Aet. 74 years.

Children of Nathaniel and Elizabeth Clapp:

John D., obt. Oct. 4, 1836. Aet. 20 mos. Mary Ann, obt. April 2, 1839. Aet. 7 mos. Jane D., obt. Jan. 4, 1841. Aet. 7 mos. John D., obt. Jan. 21, 1843. Aet. 6 yrs. Henry F., obt. Jan. 2, 1862. Aet. 27 yrs. Mary B., obt. Sept. 13, 1872. Aet. 24 yrs. Jane D., obt. Oct. 22, 1873. Aet. 19 yrs. Charles W., obt. May 17, 1876. Aet. 33 yrs.

BEDELL. x, 11. Lucy E., wife of Merrill Bedell, died Dec. 15, 1851. Aet. 33.

Wandering below who would not wish to share
The joys of heaven; leave this world of care
And join her gentle spirit, in bright realms above,
To sing forevermore His never-dying love.

HERRING. x, 12. Here lyes buried the Body of Mrs Ann Herring, the wife of Mr. James Herring; died March 9th, 1749, in ye 77th year of her age.

ELLIS. x, 13. Lyman, only son of Franklin & Marya Ellis. Jan. 7, 1856. Dec. 12, 1871.

COBURN. x, 14. In memory of two sons of Alvan & Susan Coburn. Hiram died May 4, 1830, Aet. 9 months. Alvan died June 6, 1832, Aet. 6 years.

COBURN. x, 15. Alvin Coburn died Jan. 27, 1856. Aet. 62 yrs. Hiram Coburn died June 19, 1856. Aet. 24 yrs.

KINGSBURY. x, 16. Here lie the remains of Mrs. Hannah Kingsbury, consort of Dea. Nathaniel Kingsbury. She departed this life Aug. ye 17th, 1775, in ye 76th year of her age. There is no discharge in that War.

KINGSBURY. x, 17. Here lies ye body of Mrs Elizabeth Kingsbury, the wife Deacon Nathaniel Kingsbury. She died Decr ye 20th, 1751, in ye 53^d year of her age.

KINGSBURY. x, 18. Here lie the remains of Deacon Nathaniel Kingsbury, who departed this life August ye 20th, A. D. 1775, in ye 78th year of his age.
He performed the duties of his office in the first church in Dedham for about 29 years, and having served his Generation, by the will of God he
fell asleep. Blessed are the dead who die in the Lord.

MACKERWETHY. x, 19. In memory of Mrs. Mackerwethy, who died June ye 9, 1771, in ye 77th year of her Age.

CLARK. x, 20. In memory of Abigail A., daughter of Aaron and Olive Clark: who died Oct. 27, 1831; Aet 15 yrs.
Prepare to meet thy God.

CARTER. x. 21. Mrs. Harriet Carter died Oct. 24, 1878, aged 89 years.

———RANGE XI.———

STRONG. xi, 1. William I., son of Mr. William I. & Mrs. Elleanor Strong. died July 2, 1846; aged 2 years.
Shed not for him the bitter tear,
Nor give the heart to vain regret;
'Tis but the casket that lies here;
The gem that fill'd it sparkles yet.

STRONG. xi, 2. William F., son of Mr. William I. & Mrs. Elleanor Strong, died April 25, 1844, aged 5 years & 1 mo.
Ere sin could blight, or sorrow fade,
Death came with friendly care;
The opening bud to heaven conveyed,
And bade it blossom there.

GRANT. xi, 3. Caleb Grant, son to Caleb Grant, Late of Weston, Dec^d Feby ye 10, 1731-2, in ye 20th year of his age.

HOUGHTON. xi, 4. In memory of Mr. Jesse Houghton, who died July 8, 1833. Aet. 41.

FARRINGTON. xi, 5. Abby Maria, dau. of David & Abigail Farrington, died Jan. 4, 1842. Aet. 2 years.

So fades the lovely blooming flower,   So soon our transient comforts fly,
Frail smiling solace of an hour.   And pleasure only blooms to die.

FARRINGTON. xi, 6. Oscar Ellis, only son of David & Abigail Farrington, died Dec. 22, 1838, Aet. 6 ms. & 15 ds.

FIRST PARISH.   29

> This lovely bud, so young, so fair,
> Called hence by early doom,
> Just came to show how sweet a flower
> In Paradise would bloom.

WHITING. xi, 7. Here lyes ye body of Mr. Jonathan Whiting, died Sep^t ye 4th, 1728, in ye 61st year of his age.

UPTON. xi, 8. In memory of Mr. Theodore J. Upton, who died Sept. 26, 1847, aged 35 years.

> Stop my friends as you pass by   As I am now, soon you must be
> As you are now, so once was I;   Prepare for death & follow me.

DEAN. xi, 9. John Dean 2^d, Died Sept. 30, 1847: aged 63 years.
Mrs. Betsey Dean Died Feb. 22, 1870, aged 82 yrs. 3 ms. 20 dys.

DEAN. xi, 10. Mrs. Mary Dean died Oct. 13, 1850. Aet. 98 yrs. 6 mos.

DEAN. xi, 11. John Dean died Sept. 14. 1838. Aet. 90.

RICHARDS. xi, 12. In memory of Mrs. Mary Richards, consort to Joseph
1   Richards, Esq., who Departed this life on January 1746, in the 40th year of her age.
1   Where sweetness thus and Innocence unite,
    Virtue, the Soul, and Beauty charms the Sight.
2   In memory of Joseph Richards, Esq., who departed this life on Feby 25, 1761, in the 60th year of his age.
2   My Life thou know'st is but a span, a cypher sums my years
    And every man in best estate, but vanity appears.

SCARBOROUGH. xi, 13. In memory of Mrs. Elizabeth Scarborough, who died Nov. 1, 1805. Aged 81 years.

xi, 14. Albert and Frank.

KINGSBURY. MAY. DRAPER. xi, 15. Martha T., wife of Ezekiel Kingsbury, Jr., died Aug. 26, 1829, aged 37 yrs. 4 mos. Eliza C. Kingsbury died Aug. 31, 1840, aged 23 yrs. 7 mos. 21 days. Ezekiel Kingsbury died Feb. 10, 1836, aged 68 yrs. Mary D., his wife, died Sept. 20, 1826, Aged 66 years.
Daniel May died May 29, 1819. Aged 32 years. Catherine Kingsbury, widow of Daniel May, died June 10, 1863, aged 75 years, 7 mos. 14 days. Augustus R. May died July 19, 1870, aged 56 yrs. 5 mos.
Ebenezer Draper died Jan. 3, 1784, aged 86. Dorothy, his wife, died Aug. 22, 1748, Aged 48. Sybil Avery, widow of Ebenezer Draper, died Feb. 16, 1816, aged 96 years.

HALL. PRESCOTT. xi, 16. Sabina, wife of Amos Hall. Jan. 12, 1858. Aet. 54 yrs. Amos Hall died June 26, 1863. Aet. 60 yrs. 6 mos. Mary Elizabeth, daughter of Abel and Elanor Prescott, Sept. 10, 1833. Aet. 4 yrs. Sabina Tillson, wife of Daniel H. Prescott. Dec. 4, 1852. Aet. 23 yrs. 9 mos.

WHITING. xi, 17. Loacada, wife of Abner Whiting, died Aug. 28, 1852, aged 85 yrs. 10 mos.

WHITING. xi, 18. Abner Whiting died May 20, 1838. Aged 78.
A kind husband and father and an upright and honest man.

WHITING. xi, 19. Mary, wife of Joshua Whiting, died May 25, 1825, aged 65. Mary, daughter of Joshua & Mary Whiting, died Oct. 27, 1837, aged 52.

Joshua Whiting died May 7, 1842, aged 84. Elizabeth P. Whiting died June 18, 1852, aged 56.

FARRINGTON. xi, 20. Benjamin Farrington died March 2, 1825, aged 79 years. Sarah, wife of Benjamin Farrington, died Nov. 24, 1826, aged 77 years. Simeon Farrington died June 6, 1836, aged 38 years. Eliphalet Farrington died Oct. 14, 1840, aged 62 years. Lucy P. Farrington died March 27, 1868, aged 81 yrs. 11 mos. 5 dys. James Farrington died Oct. 17, 1864, aged 82 years. Desire, wife of James Farrington, died Ap. 27, 1880, aged 87 yrs. 2 mos. & 18 days.

STOW. xi, 21. Here Lies Buried y[e] body of M[r] Nathaniel Stow. Died March 29th, 1762, in y[e] 24 year of his Age.

PAUL. xi, 22. Here lies Buried the Body of M[r] Samuel Paul, who died March 1st, 1775, in the 77th year of his age.

PAWL. xi, 23. In memory of M[rs] Abigail Pawl, wid[w] of Mr. Samuel Pawl, decea[d], who died Sept[r] 19, 1781, in the 83[d] year of her age.

DURANT. xi, 24. Here lies buried the body of Miss Faith Durant, who was driven by the hand of tyranny from Boston, the place of her nativity. She departed this life Oct. y[e] 7th, A. D. 1775. Aged 56 years.

DURANT. xi, 25. Here lie the remains of Mrs. Rachel Durant, who departed this life y[e] 7th of January, 1776, in y[e] 87th year of her age.

FALES. CHAMBERLAIN. xi, 26. Nehemiah Fales died March 14, 1857, aged 72 years. Mary, his wife died June 10, 1865. Aet. 81 yrs. 10 mos. Albion Ernest son of Charles T. and Harriet F. Chamberlain, died March 15, 1851. Aged 1 year 10 mos.

HOWE. xi, 27. Here lie the remains of Nancy Houghton Howe, dau. of M[r] Jotham & Mrs. Sally Howe, who died 18th Sept. 1796, aged 6 mos, & 10 days.

> Look here my friends, turn off your eyes
> From Earth and earthly vanities,
> And in me read your certain fate,
> That death will call you soon or late.

BERRY. xi, 28. In memory of two children of Mr. James and Mrs. Martha Berry. John died 3[d] Oct. 1800, Aet. 3 years 10 months. Caroline died 11 Oct. 1800, Aet. 1 yr. 7 mos.

> A style & temper like the saints of old,
> The mourning parents humbly wish to hold.
> These children dear no more to us shall come,
> But we must follow them down to the tomb.

WEATHERBY. xi, 29. In memory of M[rs] Submit, wife of Mr. Nathaniel Weatherby, who died March y[e] 18, A. D. 1789, in y[e] 48th year of her age.

> Here is the end of all that live,
> This is my dark long home.
> Jesus himself lay in the grave,
> The house where all must come.

BERRY. xi, 30. In memory of Mrs. Martha, wife of Mr. James Berry, who died March 2[d], 1830. Aet. 63.

The saints who now in Jesus sleep,   Till dawn the bright illustrious day,
His own Almighty power shall keep,   When death itself shall die away.

FIRST PARISH.

BERRY. xi, 31. In memory of Mr. James Berry, who died Jan. 25, 1832. Aet. 67.

HOWE. xi, 32. Isaac Howe died July 1, 1854. Aet. 53 yrs. His wife, Anne Howe, died July 15, 1874. Aet. 75 years. Isaac Francis, died Nov. 18, 1830. Aet. 4 years 8 mos. Isaac Francis, died Dec. 10, 1832. Aet. 1 year 7 mos.

CRANE. xi, 33. Sacred to the Memory of Mrs. Hannah Crane. Died May 5, 1848. Aet. 81 years.
Well done good and faithful servant.

HOWE. xi, 34. In memory of Mr. Thomas Howe, Junr, who died Decr 22, 1805. Aet. 40.

—— RANGE XII. ——

WHITING. xii, 1. Here lyes ye body of Mr. Samuel Whiting, Dec^d Jan^{ry} ye 16th, 1721-22, in ye 36th year of his age.

WHITING. xii, 2. Here lyes ye body of Mr. Samuel Whiting, aged 78 years, died Decr ye 4th, 1727.

BONNEY. xii, 3. In memory of Mrs. Deborah, wife of Mr. Seth Bonney, who died April 8, 1835, Aet. 54.

KAHLMEYER. xii, 4. Henry C. Kahlmeyer, born April 15, 1823, died Oct. 30, 1870.

LANE. xii, 5. In memory of Mrs. Hannah S., wife of Daniel Lane, jr., who died Aug. 3, 1832, Aet. 36.

KINGSBURY. xii, 6. Here lyes Buried ye Body of Mr Nathaniel Kingsbury, Dec^d Jan^{ry} ye 19th, 1724, in ye 51st year of his age.

KINGSBURY. xii, 7. Here lies the body of Mrs Abigail Kingsbury, widow of Mr Nathaniel Kingsbury. She Departed this life Novem^r 9th, 1764, in the 90th year of her age.

She lived about 20 years in single life, about 30 years in the married state, & about 40 in that of widowhood: in each of which her behavior was amiable & exemplary.
At length the aged saint comes to the tomb,
As corn when fully ripe is gathered home.

HUTCHINS. xii, 8. George H. Hutchins died Jan. 8, 1864, aged 28 years, 5 mos.
There is rest for the weary.

HUTCHINS. WHITE. SQUIRE. xii, 9. Joseph S. Hutchins died May 6, 1841, aged 45 years. Sarah Hutchins died Dec. 22, 1871, aged 72 years. George H. Hutchins, Jan. 8, 1864, aged 28 years. Luther White died Feb. 5, 1858, aged 82 years. Rebecca J. White died June 7, 1838, aged 57 years. Luther White died July 21, 1828, aged 25 years. George White died Sept. 18th, 1805, aged 2 years. Eben White died Feb. 13, 1864, aged 52 years. Sally Squire died Aug. 3, 1838, aged 63 years.

MACOMBER. xii, 10. In memory of Mr. Samuel, son of Mr. Winchester & Mrs. Polly Macomber, of Jay, Me., who died Feb. 2, 1839. Aet. 22.

Farewell, dear friend, a long farewell. We commit thy loved remains to the bosom of thy mother earth, with the joyful hope that in the morning of the resurrection thou wilt arise clothed with glory, honor, immortality, and eternal life.

FORIST. xii, 11. In memory of Miss Belinda Forist, formerly of Eaton, N. H., who died Dec. 18, 1833, Aet. 19 years.

> Farewell my friends and kindred dear,
> I've left this world of pain;
> May virtue be your practice here
> Till we shall meet again.

LEWIS. xii, 12. Mary O., dau. of John & Mary Octavia Lewis, died Sept. 30, 1843, aged 1 month.

> Sweet babe, thy sufferings all are o'er,
> In Heaven thy Spirit rests.
> A blooming rose forever more
> Upon the Savior's breast.

HOLMES. xii, 13. Eliza G., wife of Jacob B. Holmes, died June 19, 1842. Aet. 23.

> Farewell my partner and friends so dear.
> If ought on earth could keep me here,
> It sure would be my love for you,
> But Jesus calls: I bid adieu.

PAUL. xii, 14. Here lie ye body of Mrs Hannah Paul, the widow of Capt. Samuel Paul: she died Sep^t 22^d, 1748, in ye 74 year of her age.

BOWERS. xii, 15. Lewis, son of John & Catherine Bowers, died Nov. 16, 1852, Aet. 15 yrs. 10 ms. 23 ds.

FARMER. xii, 16. George P., son of C. S. & Mary Farmer, died Jan. 28, 1842, aged 11 mo^s.

BRACKET. xii, 17. Here lyes ye Body of Nathaniel Bracket, son of Mr. Anthony & Mrs. Elizabeth Bracket of Boston, aged 5 years & 8 months. Died Aug. ye 17th, 1748.

SMALL. xii, 18. Jane Elizabeth, died Oct. 16, 1833, Aet. 1 year & 10 days. Ellen Maria, died Oct. 15, 1833, Aet. 1 year & 9 days. Twin daughters of Mr. Jonathan and Mrs. Jane L. Small.

It may with propriety be said of them, they were lovely & pleasant in their lives, and in their death they were not divided.

SMALL. xii, 19. In memory of Mr. Ahira Small, who died April 10, 1836, Aet. 28.

SMALL. xii, 20. In memory of Mrs. Betsy, wife of Mr. Thomas Small, who died Feb. 27, 1838, Aet. 60.

SMALL. xii, 21. In memory of Thomas Small, who died May 24, 1854, Aet. 80.

RICHARDS. xii, 22. In memory of Albert A., son of Mr. Martin & Mrs. Harriot Richards, who died Oct. 18, 1825, Aet. 16 months.

RICHARDS. xii, 23. In memory of Mr. Martin Richards, who died Oct. 6, 1837, Aet. 41.

RICHARDS. xii, 24. Dea. Luther Richards, died Dec. 25, 1832 aged 61. Also his wife, Polly Battelle. Born Aug. 8, 1777, died Feb. 27, 1861.

> Blessed are the dead that die in the Lord.

RICHARDS. xii, 25. Alvin Richards, died Nov. 22, 1844, Aet. 28.

FIRST PARISH. 33

PHILLIPS. xii, 26. Mrs. Mehitable Phillips, died Dec. 23, 1831, Aet 31 yrs. Francis Phillips, died June 5, 1852, Aet. 31 years. Nathan Phillips, died Aug. 21, 1879, aet. 86 yrs. 1 month, 18 days.

FALES. xii, 27. Nehemiah Fales died June 6, 1800, Aet. 57. Sarah his wife died May 22, 1845, Aet. 93.

FALES. xii, 28. Sacred to the memory of Miss Elizabeth Fales, dau. of Mr. Neheh and Mrs. Sarah Fales, who was found murdered May 18th, 1801, in the 19th year of her age.

> Sainted shade of heavenly birth,
> Of matchless innocence and worth,
> Since God decreed you should be slain,
> We'll cease to mourn nor dare complain.
> Guardian Angels, watch thy swift career;
> Thy soul in Heaven will soon appear.

PARKER. xii, 29. In memory of Mr. Jonathan Parker, who died April 9, 1806, aged 37. He was a kind husband and a tender parent.

——RANGE XIII.——

JOHNSON. xiii, 1. Erected to the memory of the widow Elizabeth Johnson, who died Jan. 5, 1843, aged 52 years.

> Mother, thou hast gone and left us,
> Here thy loss we deeply feel,
> But 'tis God that hath bereft us;
> He can all our sorrows heal.

JOHNSON. xiii, 2. Mr. John Johnson died Feb. 3, 1840, Aet. 24.

> Weep not, my mother, weep not, I am blest
> But must leave heaven if I return to thee;
> For I am where the weary are at rest,
> The wicked cease from troubling:—come to me!

GRIGGS. xiii, 3. James Griggs, Born Aug. 26, 1808, died Nov. 22, 1886.

DWIGHT. xiii, 4. Here lyes Intombed the Body of Timothy Dwight Esqr, who departed this life Jan. the 31st, Anno Domini, 1718, aged 88 years. The ancestor of the Dwight family in America: A family like himself— Truly serious and godly. Of an excellent spirit, Faithful and upright, Among men of renown, In Church and State, In Halls of Learning and in War.

WALLEY. xiii, 5. James H., son of James & Ellen Walley, died Sept. 4, 1849, Aet. 10 mos.

BINGHAM. UPHAM. xiii, 6. Almira Bingham died Jan. 17, 1800, aged 18 months. Pliny Bingham, died June 6, 1840, aged 62 years. Jerusha Avery, wife of Pliny Bingham, Died Dec. 1, 1874, aged 94 yrs. Daniel Bingham died Sept. 14, 1849, aged 46 years. J. Virgil Upham, Adj. of the 102d New York Vols. Killed at Gettysburg, Pa. July 2, 1863. Aged 22 years, 0 m's 3 ds.

CODDING. xiii, 7. Adelbert A., son of Seth and Sarah Ann Codding, was drowned July 8, 1847. Aged 10 years & 11 mon's.

> The Lord had need of him.

KINGSBURY. xiii, 8. Here lyes Burried ye Body of Ensign Noah Kingsbury, dec'd Oct. 18th, 1740, in ye 47th year of his age.

RICHARDS. xiii, 9. Fanny died July 29, 1835, aged 3 years, Franklin D. died March 21, 1837, aged 17 months. Franklin D. died Sept. 8, 1841, aged 3 yrs. and 6 months. Emily C. died March 16, 1842, aged 2 yrs. and 2 months. Horace died March 22, 1842, aged 4 months
                    Children of Abiathar and Julia C. Richards:
Frank Richards died Aug. 26, 1846, aged 14 months. Abiathar Richards died Sept. 23, 1884, aged 88 years, 7 months, 10 days.

FISHER. xiii, 10. Here lies ye Body of Mrs Mary Fisher, the wife of Mr Jonathan Fisher. She died Oct. 15th, 1749, in ye 33^d year of her age.

WIGHT. xiii, 11. Here lies the Body of Mrs. Sarah Wight, the wife of Mr. Joseph Wight: She died June 28th, 1748, in ye 73 year of her age.
        [*Note.*—This Stone has been removed since 1870. C. S.]

WIGHT. xiii, 12. In memory of Dea. Joseph Wight, who died July 14, 1756, in ye 75th year of his age.
        [*Note.*—This Stone has been removed since 1870. C. S.]

GAY. xiii, 13. Here lies Buried ye Body of Mr Hezekiah Gay, who died Sept. ye 2^d, 1758. Aged 64 years & 2 months.

MASON. xiii, 14. Eliphalet F. Mason. Born Aug. 7, 1791, died July 27, 1837.
                    Children of Eliphalet and Mary F. Mason:
George Edward, born Oct. 14. 1827, died Dec. 6, 1834. George Edward, born Oct. 23, 1836, died Feb. 4, 1866. Mary F., Relict of Eliphalet F. Mason, Died June 17, 1885, aged 81 years. At the time of her death, the widow of Martin Bates.

FISHER. xiii, 15. Here lies ye Body of Mr Joseph Fisher, who departed this life July 5th, 1759, aged 47 years.

FISHER. xiii, 16. Here lies Buried the Body of Capt Josiah Fisher, who Died Feb^{ry} ye 24th, 1763, in ye 80th year of his Age.
  [*Note.*—Next is a tomb in which the body of Fisher Ames was deposited, and from which it was removed to be buried, where a monument was erected to his memory, west of the main driveway. This tomb is supposed to still contain some bodies of the Ames family.]

FALES. xiii, 17. In memory of Mr. Timothy Fales, son of Mr. Neh^{eh} & Mrs. Sarah Fales, who died Nov. 1, 1803, in the 23 year of his age.
  There is a balm for those who weep,   While the mouldering ashes sleep
      A rest for weary Pilgrims found,   —Low—in the Ground.

BADLAM. xiii, 18. Sacred to the memory of Miss Rebecca Badlam, oldest daughter of Mr. Lemuel & Mrs. Lydia Badlam, who died Sept. 3, 1810. Aged 32 years.
            Heaven only lent her for a transient hour;
              And, to secure her from the ills to come,
            Sent a bright cherub clothed with heavenly power,
              Who bore his treasure to her native home.

SEARS. xiii, 19. Sacred to the memory of Mrs. Lydia Sears, widow of the Rev. Freeman Sears of Natick, and Daug^{tr} of Mr. Lemuel & Mrs. Lydia Badlam, who died April 1st, 1814. Aged 33 years.
            As oft we to thy early urn repair
              This sweet reflection shall console the heart;
            Thy form, thy virtues deep engraven there,
              Heaven re-unites us never more to part.

FIRST PARISH.   35

BADLAM. xiii, 20. In memory of Miss Polly Badlam, youngest daug^r of Mr. Lemuel & Mrs. Lydia Badlam, died March 2d, 1815, aged 27 yrs.

<blockquote>
As oft we to thy early urn repair
This sweet reflection shall console the heart;
Thy form, thy virtues deep engraven there,
Heaven re-unites us never more to part.
</blockquote>

BADLAM. xiii, 21. In memory of Mr. Lemuel Badlam, who died Dec. 1st, 1815. Aged 60.

BADLAM. xiii, 22. In memory of Mrs. Lydia Badlam, wife of Mr. Lemuel Badlam, Died May 18, 1816. Aet. 59.

—— RANGE XIV. ——

BULLARD. xiv, 1. Here Lyes interred ye Body of Mr William Bullard, aged 73 years, 7 mon^s & 22 days, who died Febr^y ye 9th, 1746.

BULLARD. xiv, 2. Here Lyes interred ye Body of Mrs Elizabeth Bullard, ye wife of Mr William Bullard, aged 70 years, 1 month & 7 days: died Jany 28th, 1746.

BULLARD. xiv, 3. Here Lyes ye Body of Mr William Bullard, jun^r, who died 19th Sept., 1737, in ye 40 year of his Age.

AVERY. xiv, 4. Here Lyes buried ye Body of Mrs Elizabeth Avery, widow of Ensign Robert Avery. She died Oct. ye 21st, A. D. 1746, in ye 91st year of her Age.

AVERY. xiv, 5. Here lyes Buried ye Body of Robert Avery, jun^r, who Dec^d August ye 21st, 1723, in ye 42^d year of his age.

AVERY. xiv, 6. Here lyes buried ye Body of Ensign Robert Avery, who dec^d Octr ye 4, 1722, in ye 73^d year of His Age.

CROSBY. xiv, 7. Edmund Crosby died March 3, 1875, aged 70 yrs. Rachel A., his wife, died July 9, 1859, aged 51 yrs.

METCALF. xiv, 8. Here lyes ye Body of Samuel Metcalf, son to Mr Thomas & M^{rs}. Sarah Metcalf, who died June, 1713, in ye 15 year of his Age.

METCALF. xiv, 9. Here lyes ye Body of Thomas Metcalf, aged 25 years. Died December 28, 1726.

METCALF. xiv, 10. Jonat^a Metcalf, the son of Mr. Jonathan & Mrs. Elizabeth Metcalf. He Died May 22, 1749. Aged 5 months.

METCALF. xiv, 11. Here lies the Body of Elias Metcalf, 8th son & 13th child to Mr John & Mrs Mary Metcalf, died Jany 15th, 1753, in ye 11th year of his age.

METCALF. xiv, 12. Joseph, son of Joseph & Rebecca Metcalf, died Aug. 26, 1799, aged 4 years.

METCALF, xiv, 13. In memory of Capt. Reuben Metcalf, who died Aug. 13, 1842, aged 45 years. Hannah S. Metcalf died Feb. 15, 1881, aged 84 years.

<blockquote>
Farewell conflicting joys and fears,
Where lights and shades alternate dwell,
A brighter, purer, scene appears,
Farewell, inconstant world farewell.
</blockquote>

METCALF. xiv, 14. In memory of Augusta Lyman, daughter of Reuben and Hannah Metcalf, who died Dec. 8, 1838; aged 6 years & 8 months.

Adieu, Dear Augusta, too tender, too pure
To inhabit this cold world of sorrow & pain;
To regions of bliss thy young spirit has flown,
To join thy lost brothers in loves purest reign.

METCALF. xiv, 15. In memory of Lyman Augustus, son of Reuben and Hannah Metcalf, who died March 29, 1830, aged 5 years and 2 months.

Ere sin could blight, or sorrow fade,
Death timely came with friendly care,
The opening bud to heaven conveyed
And bade it bloom forever there.

METCALF. xiv, 16. In memory of John Smith Metcalf, son of Reuben and Hannah Metcalf, who died June 3, 1838; aged 15 years.

Dear boy for him each sport is o'er,
He joins the jocund band no more;
Pillowed beneath this little heap,
Mirth cannot break his dreamless sleep.
Come, to this spot repair
And while we mourn grow better here;
Here humbly bow to natures awful lot,
To live, to suffer, die, and be forgot.

METCALF. xiv, 17. Here lyes Buried ye body of Mr Thomas Metcalf. Died September ye 22^d, 1704, in ye 34 year of his age.

METCALF. xiv, 18. Here lyes ye Body of Deacon Thomas Metcalf. Aged 73 years. Died Novemb^r ye 16, 1702.

METCALF. xiv, 19. Here lyes Buried ye Body of Mrs. Elizabeth Metcalf, ye wife of Mr. Jonathan Metcalf, who died May ye 14, 1765, in ye 45th year of her Age.

METCALF. xiv, 20. Here lies buried the body of John Metcalf, Esqr., who departed this life Oct. ye 6th, A. D. 1749, in the 72^d year of his Age.

METCALFE. xiv, 21. Here lyes ye Body of Mrs Katharine Metcalfe, second daug^r of Mr John Metcalfe, Esq. She died June ye 12, 1746. Aged 24 years.

METCALFE. xiv, 22. Here lies ye Body of Mrs Sarah Metcalfe, dau^r of John Metcalfe, Esqr & Mrs Grace, his wife. She died Sep^t. 3^d, 1749, in ye 23 year of Her Age.

METCALFE. xiv, 23. Here lies ye Body of Mrs Grace Metcalfe, J^{sr}, Daur. of John Metcalfe, Esqr & Mrs Grace, his wife: She died Aug. 13th, 1749, in ye 17 year of Her Age.

METCALF. xiv, 24. In memory of Mr. Joseph Metcalf, who died Feb. 25, 1785: Aged 75 years. Also his wife Ruth, who died March 3d, 1803, aged 76 years.

METCALF. xiv, 25. Here lyes ye Body of Timothy Metcalf, 3^d son of John & Mehetabel Metcalf. Died August 14th, 1727, in ye 20th year of his age.

METCALF. xiv, 26. Here lies buried ye Body of Deacon Jonathan Metcalf, who died May ye 23^d, 1727, in ye 77th year of his age.

METCALF. xiv, 27. Joseph died Oct. 26, 1857, aged 92 years, 6 mos. 6 days. His wife, Rebecca Metcalf, died Sep, 26, 1848, aged 84 yrs., 4 mos.

TURNER. xiv, 28. Lavina R., wife of Francis Turner, died Sept. 7, 1852.

Aet. 32. Francis E., son of Francis & Amelia B. Turner, died Nov. 5, 1885. Aet. 3 mos. 13 days. Also Amelia L., died Aug. 26, 1859. Aet. 10 mos.

AVERY. xiv, 29. William Avery died March 18, 1686, aged 66. William Avery died December 15, 1708, aged 62. William Avery died A. D. 1756, aged 85. William Avery died August 6, 1796, aged 80. Bethia, his wife, died December 25, 1793, aged 78. William died February 15, 1798, aged 55. Jonathan Avery died February 11, 1833, aged 88. Jerusha, his wife, died March 25, 1822, 77. William Avery died November 3, 1791, aged 21. Daniel Avery died Sept. 3, 1793, aged 5. Lucy Avery died April 30, 1824, aged 39.

BOSWORTH, xiv, 30. Asaph, son of Asaph and Martha O. Bosworth, died Jan. 12, 1835. Aet. 3 y's, 9 mo. & 12 days.

HOUGHTON. xiv, 31. Charles L., son of Ephraim & Polly Houghton, died Jan. 28, 1836. Aet. 3 yrs. 1 mo. & 18 ds.

See the lovely blooming flower, So our transient comforts fly,
Fade and wither in an hour; Pleasure only blooms to die.

RICHARDS. xiv, 32. In memory of Mrs. Rebecca Richards, wife to Mr. Samuel Richards, daughter to Capt. Joshua & Mrs. Hannah Fisher, dec^d May ye 25th, 1740. Aged 30 years, 5 months & 3 days.

HOUGHTON. xiv, 33. E. Houghton, 1795—1879. P. Houghton, 1807—1872. C. L. Houghton, 1832—1836. C. E. Houghton, 1838—1839. Wm Houghton, 1788—1868,

FISHER. DIX. xiv, 34. Paul Fisher died Oct. 23, 1846, aged 73 yrs. Lavina, wife of Paul Fisher, died June 2, 1875, aged 92 yrs. 9 mos. Nathaniel Fisher Dix died Sept. 15, 1845, aged 13 months.

Blessed are the dead who die in the Lord.

MORRELL. xiv, 35. Eliakim Morrell died Aug. 13, 1824, aged 71 years. Ruth Morrell died Sept. 8, 1824, aged 74 yrs. Isaac Morrell died Aug. 18, 1833, aged 10 weeks. Abner Morrell died June 30, 1840, aged 16 yrs, Nancy W. Morrell died Jan. 16, 1846, aged 18 years. Joseph Morrell died Sept. 7, 1867, aged 77 yrs. Nancy Morrell died June 3, 1876, aged 80 years.

SOUTHWORTH. xiv, 36. In memory of Mrs. Hannah Southworth. Obt. Nov. 2, 1831. Aet. 35.

Precious in the sight of the Lord is the death of his Saints.

SMITH. xiv, 37. In memory of Mr. Samuel Smith, who died 6th Nov., 1802. Aged 56 years.
Death is a Debt to Nature due,
I have paid it & so must you.

DUNTIN. xiv, 38. In memory of Mrs. Ruth Duntin, who died 19 May, 1802. Aet. 77 years.
Now is Christ risen from the dead and become the first fruit of them who slept.

POMEROY. xiv, 39. In memory of two children of Mr. Zadock & Mrs. Hannah Pomeroy of Boston. Arabella died Nov. 17, 1801, aged 2 years and 9 months. George died Dec. 2, 1801, aged 11 months & 20 days.

FARRINGTON. xiv, 40. In memory of Mr. Stephen Farrington, who died Aug. 13, 1831. Aet. 60.

FARRINGTON. xiv, 41. William Farrington, son of Stephen & Mrs. Lucy Farrington, who died Sept. 17, 1801, aged 1 year & 4 months.

So fades the lovely blooming flower,   So soon our transient comforts fly,
Frail Smiling solace of an hour,   And pleasure only blooms to die.

FARRINGTON. xiv, 42. In memory of Mrs. Lucy Farrington, who died Sept. 24, 1842. Aet. 73.

FARRINGTON. xiv, 43. Aunt Charlotte (Charlotte Farrington), 1708—1878.

EDSON. xiv, 44. In memory of Mr. Robert Edson, who died Feb. 11, 1841, aged 51 years.

EDSON. xiv, 45. Infant son of Mr. Robert & Mrs. Esther G. Edson, born and died Oct. 12, 1836.

BADLAM. xiv, 46. In memory of Mr. William Badlam, died July 22, 1818. Aet. 92.

EDSON. xiv, 47. In memory of Mrs. Betsey, wife of Mr. Robert Edson, who died June 7, 1835, aged 51 years.

SMITH. xiv, 48. In memory of Mr. Daniel Smith, who died 6 Nov. 1802, aged 56 years.

Death is a debt to nature due
That I have paid & so must you.

DAMON. xiv, 49. Memory of Mr. John Damon, who died Nov. 3, 1792, in the 62d year of his age.

The sweet remembrance of the Just,   A train of blessings for his heirs,
Like a green root, revives and bears When dying nature sleeps in dust.

ONION. xiv, 50. In memory of Mr. Joseph Onion, who died 6 Dec. 1792, aged 37 years.

BICKFORD. xiv, 51. Willard T. Bickford, died Oct. 27, 1841. Aet. 19.

——RANGE XV.——

MUSCHE. xv, 1. Isabella Musche died July 24th, 1875. Aged 4 months.

STRONG. xv, 2. Ann Eliza, dau. of John & Lydia Strong, died Apr. 26, 1842. Aet. 1 year, 8 ms,

HIRSCH. xv, 3. In memory of Geo. S. Hirsch, died June 19, 1876. Aged 43 yrs., 8 mos.

ALLIN. ADAMS. BELCHER. DEXTER. HAVEN. BATES. LAMSON. xv, 4. (East Side). Rev. John Allin, First Pastor of Dedham. Born in 1596. Entered the Ministry in England. Came over in 1637. The same year Joined the company at Dedham. Ordained Pastor April 24, 1639. Died August 26, 1671. A man of signal worth Of unaffected piety, And great evenness of disposition. Prudent, meek, patient and serene. He faithfully fed his flock. And by his writings and counsels obtained a wide-spread reputation, And rendered eminent service to the N. E. Colonies.

(North side). Successors of Mr. Allin gone to their rest before the erection of this monument:

Rev. Willliam Adams, b. May 27, 1650. Grad. H. C. 1671. Ord. Dec. 3, 1673; died Aug. 17, 1685.

Rev. Joseph Belcher b. 1671. Grad. H. C. 1690. Ord. Nov. 29, 1693; died Apl 27, 1723.

Rev. Samuel Dexter, b. at Malden Oct. 25, 1700. Grad. H. C. 1720; Ord. May 6, 1724. died Jan. 29, 1755.

FIRST PARISH. 39

Rev. Jason Haven, b. at Framingham, March 2, 1733. Grad. H. C. 1754. Ord. Feb. 5, 1756. died May 17, 1803.

Rev. Joshua Bates, D. D. b. at Cohasset 20. March, 1776. Grad. H. C. 1800. Ord. 16 March, 1803; left for the Presidency of Middlebury College, Vt. 20th Feb. 1818; d. 14 Jan. 1854.

(South side). Church gathered Nov. 8, 1638.

Rev. Alvan Lamson, D. D. Born at Weston Nov. 18, 1792. Grad. H. C. 1814. Ord. Oct. 28, 1818. Resigned Oct. 20, 1860. Died July 18, 1864.

(East side). Erected in 1854 by residents within the old territorial Parish.

AVERY. xv, 5. (Mary) Avery, aged 20 years, dec'd October ye 11, 1681.

[*Note.*—This stone is broken, but the foot-stone has on it the name Mary Avery. C. S.]

AVERY. xv, 6. Here Lyes ye body of Deacon William Avery, aged 62 years. Died December ye 15, 1708.

FOX. xv, 7. Thomas Fox, ye son of Jabez & Judeth Fox, aged about 18 years, died July ye 29, 1699.

TURNER. xv, 8. Ebenezer Turner died Aug. 5, 1858. Aged 73 yrs. 3 ms. 7 days. Sally, his wife, died Jan. 12, 1858. aged 71 years, 10 mos. 19 days. James Turner died Feb. 12, 1825, aged 70 years. Jemima, his widow, died Sep. 14, 1856, aged 99 years, 10 mos. 7 days. Danford Turner died June 14, 1802, aged 5 yrs. 7 mos. Joel Turner died Oct. 21, 1813, aged 31 years, 5 mos. 8 days.

CURTIS. xv, 9. Hannah, wife of E. H. Curtis, died Aug. 9, 1870, aged 46 years. 5 mos.

The Lord is my Shepard.

NOYES. CUMMINGS. xv, 10. Mary A. Noyes died June 7, 1842. Aet. 14 years. Polly Cummings Died Dec. 18, 1863. Aet. 83. Nancy G., wife of Otis Noyes, died Sept. 16, 1874. Aet. 71 years. Otis Noyes died June 23, 1878. Aet. 76 years.

DEAN. xv, 11. Louis E., son of W^m and A. Dean, died Jan. 8, 1839. Aet. 3 yrs. 4 mos. 24 days.

DEAN. xv, 12. Joseph Dean, Jr., died Feb. 19, 1814. Aet. 39. Mrs. Hannah, his wife, died Oct. 16, 1843. Aet. 67.

NOYES. xv, 13. Hannah Noyes died Oct. 8, 1801, aged 1 year, 3 months. Hannah Noyes died Oct. 31, 1823. aged 18 years. Nathaniel Noyes died March 23, 1829, aged 55 years. Catherine, wife of Nathaniel Noyes, died Jan. 13, 1859, aged 83 years.

DEAN. xv, 14. Mary Ann, daug^t of Mr. Josiah and Mrs. Mary Dean, died Oct 18, 1821. Aet. 6 years.

JACKSON. xv, 15. Lucy, wife of M B. Jackson, died Oct. 7, 1856, aged 37 years.

DEAN. xv, 16. Josiah Dean died Aug. 5, 1842, aged 64 years, 1 mo. 22 days. Mary, wife of Josiah Dean, died April 20, 1852, aged 73 y. 11 m. 15 d. Elizabeth B. Dean d. Feb. 22, 1877, aged 69 y. 6 m. 8 d.

WOODS. xv, 17. Emmeline Mary, wife of Charles Woods & dau of Seth & Alice Sumner, died Apr. 16, 1840. Aet. 33.

Born by a new Celestial birth,   For, Strangers into life we come;
Why should we grovel here on earth;   And dying is but going home.

SUMNER. xv, 18. Sacred to the memory of Mr. Seth Sumner, who died July 16, 1827, aged 53 years. Also Alice Sumner, who died April 12th, 1828, aged 14 years. Eliza Sumner died Oct' 9th, 1821. Aged 4 years. Daughters of Mr. Seth Sumner & Alice his wife.

POLLARD. xv, 19. Sacred to the memory of Col. Jonathan Pollard, who departed this life 12. Feb. 1802, in the 53 year of his age.

BULLARD. xv, 20. Abba, wife of John Bullard, died Oct. 26, 1848. Aet. 87.

BULLARD. xv, 21, In memory of John Bullard, who died Jan'y 3, 1800, aged 48 years.

BULLARD. xv, 22. In memory of Dea. Isaac Bullard, who died 18. June, 1808. Aet. 64.

If we believe that Jesus died and rose again, Even so them also which sleep in Jesus will God bring with him.

BULLARD. xv, 23. In memory of Mrs. Patience Bullard, who died 16th Nov. 1819. Aet. 75.

Hail glorious Gospel heavenly light whereby
We live with comfort and with comfort die.

———RANGE XVI.———

STONE. xvi, 1. In memory of Daniel Stone, who died Aug"t 22d, 1815. Aet. 24 years. Only son of Daniel & Sarah Stone.
Blessed are they who die in the Lord.

ALGER. JOHNSON. BUTRICK. POYEN. HARGRAVES. xvi, 2. Betsey E. Alger, died Feb. 26, 1846, aged 37 years. Alfred Johnson, died April 10, 1860, aged 23 yrs. 3 mos. Mrs. Eliza Jane, wife of William H. Butrick, died at Haverhill, Mass., May 31, 1861. Aged 27. years. Louis F. Poyen, Lieut. 1st Batt. Mass. Heavy Artillery, died March 26, 1866, aged 28 years. Noel M. Johnson, died May 15, 1871, aged 63 years. Annie L. Johnson. died Feb. 17, 1874, aged 18 years. Lucy A. Hargraves died Jan. 4, 1877, a. 1 year 21 days. Mrs. Lucy A. Johnson, wife of Noel M. Johnson, died Sept. 3, 1887, aged 78 years 11 mo. & 7 days.

RICHARDS. xvi, 3. Here lyes Buried y° body of Mr. Nathaniel Richards, aged 78 years, dec'd February y° 15th 1726-7.

FISHER. xvi, 4. Here Lyes y° body of Mrs Margaret Fisher, dau' to Mr John and Mrs Mary Fisher, aged 25 years & 10 months. Dec'd Feb'y y° 2d 1735.

RICHARDS. xvi, 5. Here Lyes Buried the Body of Sarah Richards, wife to Corn't Edward Richards, aged 43 years. Dec'd Feb'y y° 22d, 1732.

ELLIS. xvi, 6. Here Lyes y° Body of Ensign Joseph Ellis, aged about 55 years. Dec'd Nov' y° 18th, 1721.

WHITING. xvi, 7. Here Lyes y° Body of Mr Timothy Whiting, died Dec' y° 26th, 1728, in y° 75 year of his age.

FISH. xvi, 8. Ebenezer Fish died July 8, 1845, aged 1 yr. 14 dys. Abbie B. Fish, died Dec. 12, 1851. Aet. 1 yr. 1 mo. James F. Fish died Mar. 17, 1853. Aet. 32 yrs. Frances M. Fish d. Dec. 2, 1880. Aet. 60 yrs. Susan Frances Fish died May 12. 1836. Aet. 1 yr. 6 ms. Abbie Barnes Fish, died Jan. 1, 1837, aet. 1

day. Ebenezer Fish died Ap. 10, 1837. Aet. 27 years. Sarah H. Fish died Jan. 13, 1848. Aet. 26 years. Eli Fish died Jan. 24, 1849. Aet. 65 yrs.

RICHARDS. xvi, 9. Thaddeus Richards, son to Mr Edward and M^n Hannah Richards. Aged 5 years, 11 m^o & 5 D^s. Dec^d May ye 22^d, 1747.

RICHARDS. xvi, 10. Here lies ye Body of Edward Richards, son of Lieut. Edward Richards & Hannah, his wife, aged 12 years, 9 months & 7 days. Died Jany 25, 1750-1.

SMITH. xvi, 11. Nathaniel Smith died Oct. 3, 1861, aged 74 years. Betsey Ford Smith died Dec. 12, 1843, aged 51 years. Two infant twin sisters, children of N. & B. F. S., died Mch 30, 1822. James Foord, son of N. &. B. F. S., died Jan. 29, 1826, aged 0 years.

SMITH. xiv, 12. In memory of Mrs. Nancy Smith, wife of Mr. Nathaniel Smith, who died Sept. 25th, 1814, in the 52^d year of her age.

SMITH. xvi, 13. In memory of Mr. Nathl Smith, who died March 3^d, 1813, in the 55th year of his age.

SMITH. xvi, 14. In memory of Miss Margaret, daughter of Nathl & Nancy Smith, who died Dec. 26, 1817, aged 32.

SMITH. xvi, 15. In memory of Mr. William Smith, who died Decr 2^d. 1811. In his 58th year.

WEATHERBEE. xvi, 16. In memory of Mr. Comfort Weatherbee, who died Sept. 4, 1812. Aet. 48. Also Mrs. Rene, his wife, died Nov. 7, 1838. Aet. 63.

ATHERTON. xvi, 17. Catherine, wife of Abner Atherton, died Oct. 15, 1811, Aet. 33. Abner Atherton, died Dec. 24, 1847, Aet. 72. Betsey, wife of Abner Atherton, died Aug. 16, 1849. Aet. 66.

FROST. xvi, 18. In memory of John H. Frost, son of Mr. John & Mrs. Fanny Frost, who died June 26, 1820. Aet. 11. weeks.

    Behold the mother's eye—a tear   While on the sable bier
    Steals silently along.   Her only son is borne.

[*Note.*—This stone has been removed since 1870. C. S.]

FISHER. xvi, 19. Hannah Fisher, died Aug. 29, 1849. Aet. 60. Hannah M. Fisher, died Mar. 22, 1852. Aet. 23. Billings Fisher, died Feb. 5, 1854. Aet. 73.

RICHARDS. xvi, 20. In memory of Mr. Reuel Richards, who died in Smithfield, R. I., Nov. 18, 1838. Aet. 51.

    Lover and friend where hast thou fled,
    Why art thou slumbering with the dead?
    Companion of my youth!
    From me by death thou art removed
    And from the children you dearly loved.
    Can it be so? 'tis truth.
    Upon Thine arm, Almighty King.
    Permit my widowed heart to lean;
    In thee I put my trust.

RICHARDS. xvi, 21. In memory of Mrs. Elizabeth Richards, who died April 10, 1848, Aet. 88.

    Light is sown for the righteous,
    And goodness for the upright in heart.

RICHARDS. xvi, 22. In memory of Mr. Abiathar Richards, who died July 10, 1835. Aet. 81.
There remaineth therefore a rest to the people of God.

RICHARDS. xvi, 23. Catharine Richards, died January 4, 1887, aged 80 yrs. 6 mos. 17 days.

COLBURN. xvi, 24. Here lies ye Body of Mr. Benjamin Colburn, who died Augt 15, 1747. Aged 58 years 2 months & 18 days.

RICHARDS. xvi, 25. Here lies ye Body of Mrs. Hannah Richards, wife of Lieu^t Edward Richards. Died Jan^{ry} ye 4th, 1755, in the 56th year of her age.

RICHARDS. xvi, 26. Here lies Interred the Remains of Lieu^t Edward Richards, who died Decem^r 3^d, 1771. Aged 87 years,

FULLER. xvi, 27. Here lies ye Body of Mr Hezekiah Fuller, who departed this life July 8, 1756, in ye 69 year of his age.

COBB. xvi, 28. In memory of Calvin Cobb, (only son of Mr. Daniel & Mrs. Mary Cobb.) aged 7 years, who was instantly killed by the discharge of a musket April 30, 1829.

> Oh! hapless parents, who shall paint your woe
> On viewing this your lovely child laid low,
> Whose budding virtues just began to bloom
> Ere he was summoned to this early tomb.
> Our Heavenly Father takes his children home
> To save them, doubtless, from the ills to come.

FULLER. xvi, 29, Enoch Fuller, died Mar. 1, 1823. Aet. 46.

IVERS. xvi, 30. Samuel Ivers, born Feb. 26, 1795, died Mar. 10, 1860. Caroline F., wife of Samuel Ivers, born Mar. 6, 1802, died May 20, 1853.

BURGESS. xvi, 31. Abbie P. Burgess, Born Aug. 26, 1854, Died Apr. 24, 1855. Carrie Frances, wife of Ebenezer P. Burgess, Died Jan. 3, 1859, Aged 29 years.   Blessed are the dead that die in the Lord.

PAUL. DICKERMAN. ALDEN. FALES. SWAN. xvi, 32. William Paul, died February 14, 1816, aged 52 years. Anna Dickerman, died April 7, 1851, Aet. 84. Adeline Alden, died Dec. 12, 1834. Aet. 32 years.   Leonard Alden, died Oct. 27, 1871, Aet. 78 years. 10 months. Samuel Fales, died Sept. 20, 1834, Aet. 88. Rebecca Fales, died Sept. 18, 1830, Aet. 83. Joseph Swan, died Nov. 13, 1818, Aet. 45 years. Nancy, wife of Joseph Swan, died Jan. 1, 1839, aged 68 years. Joseph Warren Swan, died Sept. 25, 1838, Aet. 29 years.

BULLARD. xvi, 33. Charles Bullard, born August 13, 1794, died July 29, 1871.

BULLARD. xvi, 34. William Bullard Died March 15, 1803, aged 33 years. Lydia Bullard, widow of William Bullard, Died Nov. 24, 1859. Aged 88 years.

WHITING. xvi, 35. In memory of Mrs. Lydia Whiting, widow of Mr. William Whiting, who died Sept. 26, 1802. Aged 57 years.

> My flesh must slumber in the ground
> Till the last trumpets joyful sound
> Then burst the chains in sweet surprise
> And in my Savior's image rise.

MASON. xvi, 36. In memory of Mr. John Mason of Sturbridge, who died July 30th, 1803. In the 25th year of his age.

FIRST PARISH.

Stop my friend as you pass by
As you are now so once was I.
As I am now so you must be
Prepare for Death & follow me.

WHITING. xvi, 37. In memory of Mr. William Whiting who died 26 Jan. 1801, in the 60 year of his age.

Friends nor physicians could not save
My mortal body from the grave.
Nor can the grave confine it there,
When Christ doth call it to appear.

WHITING. xvi, 38. In memory of two children of M^r W^m & Mrs Lydia Whiting. Viz, Joe died Sept. 15, 1792, Aet. 19. James died July 16, 1793, Aet. 4.

Behold and see, my former mates
My name's engraved on this plate.
Pray think of me when this you see
You'r not far from eternity.

——RANGE XVII.——

STOWELL. xvii, 1. Joel Stowell died June 3, 1858. Aet. 84 years.

STOWELL. xvii, 2. In memory of Sarah Stowell who died at Boston Dec. 10, 1826, Aet. 46.

DRAKE. xvii, 3. Sarda Drake died July 11, 1828, aged 47: Polly Drake, wife of Sarda Drake, died Nov. 22, 1830, aged 56.

CLARK. xvii, 4. In memory of Mr. Spencer W. Clark who died Feb. 28 1841. Aet. 63.

SMITH. xvii, 5. Abner Smith died Mar. 29, 1871, aged 84.
An honest man's the noblest work of God.
Fanny Smith, Sept. 4, 1784, Jan. 31, 1874.
She hath done what she could.

SCHOPF. xvii, 6. Barbara Schopf died in E. Dedham Jan. 11th, 1878. Ae. 51 yrs. 1 mo,

COBHAM. xvii, 7. Here Lyeth ye body of Josiah Cobham aged about 24 years. Died April ye 8, 1701.

LYONS. xvii, 8. In memory of Mrs. Mary, wife of Mr. John Lyons, who died May. 1825, aged 34. Also of his 2^d wife, Mrs. Mary J., who died April 11, 1852, aged 67 years.

Jesus can make a dying bed
Feel soft as downy pillows are.
While on his breast I lean my head
And breathe my life out sweetly there.

NASON. xvii, 9. In memory of Miss Clarissa H. Nason who died July 22, 1834, aged 30 years.

McWHIRK. xvii, 10. In memory of John son of Alexander & Matilda McWhirk, who died Sept. 11, 1829, agea 2 yrs. 10 mos.

BULLARD. THOMPSON. xvii, 11. Jesse Bullard died Sept. 29, 1821, aged 1 yr. 6 mos. Harriet Bullard died Jan. 3, 1828, aged 16 years. Children of Willard and Harriet Bullard.

Harriet Bullard died Jan. 10, 1835, aged 46 years. Willard Bullard died Aug. 12, 1859, aged 72 years. Susan, widow of Willard Bullard, died Mar. 2, 1871, aged 82.

Mrs. Sibel Thompson died Jan. 30, 1834, aged 70 years. Formerly of Medfield.

Smith. xvii, 12. In memory of Mr. Lemuel Smith, who died March 29 1822. Aet. 62.

Smith. xvii, 13. In memory of Mrs. Susanna, wife of Mr. Lemuel Smith who died April 3, 1835, Aet. 76.

> Why do we mourn departing friends
> Or shake at death's alarms,
> 'Tis but the voice that Jesus sends
> To call us to his arms.

Bird. xvii, 14. Walter F., son of Francis & Emily Bird, died Sept. 2, 1852. Aet. 4 months.

Woods. xvii, 15. Mary Isabella Woods, died July 26, 1842. Aet. 1 week, Mary A., wife of William G. Woods, died July 20, 1852, aet. 38. Mrs. Caroline A., wife of Wm. G. Woods, died June 7, 1862. Aet. 42 yrs. 9 mos. Wm. G. Woods, died Oct. 3, 1863. Aet. 47 years.

Trask. xvii, 16. Erected in memory of Mr. Luke Trask who departed this life May 11th 1811 in his 29th year.

Dewolf. xvii, 17. Hannah, wife of Nathan Dewolf, died Dec. 10, 1862, Aet. 76 ys. 9 ms.

> Oh happy day that fixed my choice
> On thee, my Savior and my God.

Dewolf. xvii, 18. In memory of Mr. Nathan Dewolf, who died Decr 5th 1811, in his 32^d year.

> There is a balm for those who weep,
> A rest for weary pilgrims found;
> While the mouldring ashes sleep.
> Low —— in the ground.

Talbot. xvii, 19. Mrs. Martha Talbot, wife of Mr. Nathaniel Talbot, died Nov. 18, 1824. Æ. 76.

> While fond affection sheds the frequent tear
> O'er the cold form that rests beneath this sod;
> Hope sweetly whispers that the soul sincere
> Reposes on the bosom of her God.

Talbot. xvii, 20. In memory of Mr. Nathaniel Talbot, who died Oct. 17, 1820, aged 81.

> Forgive, blest shade, the tributary tear
> That mourns thy exit from a world like this,
> Forgive the wish that would have kept thee here,
> And stayed thy progress to the seats of bliss.
> No more confined to grovling scenes of night,
> No more a tenant pent in mortal clay.
> Now should we rather hail thy glorious flight,
> And trace thy journey to the realms of day.

Stowell. xvii. 21. Hannah, daughter of Jesse & Mary Stowell, died June 13, 1840. Aet. 22. Jesus wept.

Talbot. xvii, 22. Lucy Talbot died Apr. 3, 1842. Aet. 58.

> Blessed are the dead who die in the Lord.

FIRST PARISH.   45

TALBOT. xvii, 23.   Josiah Talbot died May 2, 1847. Aet. 65.
Be ye also ready.

COLBURN. xvii, 24, George L., son of Lyman R. & Joea Colburn, died Sept. 19, 1837. Aet. 10 ms. & 21 ds.

DANIEL. SHUMWAY. xvli, 25. Jesse Daniel died Aug. 20, 1832. Aet. 46 years. Nancy S., daughter of Jesse & Mary Daniell, died Oct. 11, 1833: Aet. 17 months. Mary, wife of Jesse Daniell, died Nov. 19, 1865. Aet. 77 years. Mary, wife of Erastus Shumway, died April 28, 1839. Aet. 21 years. Alvin J., son of Erastus & Mary Shumway, died March 11, 1842. Aet. 3 years. Erastus Shumway died June 8, 1851. Aet. 40 years.
He that hath pity upon the poor, lendeth unto the Lord.

Erastus D. Shumway died Feb. 11, 1855. Aet. 3 yrs. 7 mos.

RICHARDS. xvii, 26. Here lyes Buried ye Body of Mr Nathaniel Richards who died Oct. ye 25th, 1749, in ye 70th year of his age.

HOWE. xvii, 27. Calvin Newton, son of Calvin and Polly Howe, died Nov. 12, 1825; Ae. 8 months.

HOWE. xvii, 28. Sacred to the memory of Mr. Calvin Howe, who died June 27, 1829. Aet. 30 years.

HOWE. xvii, 29. Polly, wife of Calvin Howe. Born May 28, 1795. Died May 21, 1864.

RICHARDS. xvii, 30. Here lies Buried ye Body of Mr Jonathan Richards, who died Sepr 4th, 1750, aged 48 years 2 months & 20 days.

RICHARDS. xvii, 31. In memory of Mr. James Richards, who died May 22^d, 1760. Ae. 77 years. Mrs. Hannah Richards, wife of Mr. James Richards, who died Feby 8th, 1770. Ae. 83 yrs.
The memory of the Just is Blessed.

The saints though buried in the dust,   Surviving friends, O drop a tear,
Shall rise again among the just.   Remember your own death is near.

SMITH. xvii, 32. In memory of Mr. Josiah Smith who died March, 1765, aet 80 years.

BAKER. xvii, 33. In memory of M^r. Joseph Baker who died March ye 1st, 1765, in ye 75th year of his age. In memory of Mrs Hannah Baker, wife of Mr Joseph Baker, who died Aug. 2, 1763, in ye 73^d of her age.

DAMON. xvii, 34. Here lyes Buried ye Body of Mrs Hopestill Damon, ye wife of Mr Joseph Damon, who died January ye 31st, 1770, in ye 39 year of her Age, Also Mary Damon, her child, Age 3, days.

WILLSON. xvii, 35. Here lies Buried the Body of Deacon Ephraim Willson, ob^t July 19th, 1769, in the 80th year of his age.

WILLSON. xvii. 36. In memory of Mrs Hannah, (wife of Dea. Ephraim Willson) who died Augst ye 6th, 1776, in ye 70th year of her age.

——RANGE XVIII.——

HAYWARD. xviii, 1. Here Lieth Buried Mary, Y^e wife of John Hayward, aged 68 years. Died April the 24th, 1684.

FORD. xviii, 2. Sacred to the memory of John Ford, died Nov. 17, 1874, aged 20 years, 2 mos. Agnes Ford died Oct. 7, 1875, aged 1 year 11 mos. James Ford died Mar. 13, 1876, aged 9 yrs. 10 mos.

SWEET. xviii, 3. In memory of Miss Elizabeth, daugh^{tr} of Mr. Rufus & Mrs. Elizabeth Sweet! of No. Kingston, R. I., who departed this life Aug. 31, 1826. Aet. 23 Y. 11 M. 6 D.

> In youthful bloom death laid me down
> Here to await the trumpets sound:
> Till God shall bid my dust arise,
> To meet my Savior in the skies.
> Stand still, kind reader, drop one tear
> Over the dust that slumbers here;
> And when you read the state of me;
> Think of the glass that runs for thee.

RITZ. xviii, 4. Here lies in peace Maria C. Ritz, who died Oct. 4th, 1878. Aged 67 years.

WELCH. xviii, 5. In memory of Mr. Joel Welch, who died Oct. 27, 1827. In his 24th year.

JACKMAN. xviii, 6. In memory of Miss Martha Jackman, who died Feb. 9, 1833. Aet. 23.

CROOKER. xviii, 7. Little Gerty, born April 11th, 1874, died Novr 30th, 1877, aged 3 yrs. 7 mos. 19 d's. daughter of Calvin B, and Maria F. Crooker.

CALDWELL. xviii, 8. Miss Mary, dau. of Mr. John & Mrs. Nancy Caldwell, died May 12, 1845. Aged 17 years.

> See the fair cheek of beauty fade,
> Frail glory of an hour:
> And blooming youth with sickening head
> Droop like the dying flower.

[*Note.*—This stone has been removed since 1870.—C. S.]

SHUTTLEWORTH. xviii, 9. Jeremiah Shuttleworth, born Dec. 25, 1760, died June 7, 1841. Aet. 80. Sukey Shuttleworth, his wife, born April 16, 1779, died Oct. 3, 1800. Henry Shuttleworth, born Feb. 29, 1804, died Feb. 14, 1806. Samuel Shuttleworth, born Dec. 2, 1807, died Ap. 6, 1864. Jeremiah Shuttleworth, born May 17, 1802, died June 13, 1872. Hannah Shuttleworth, born Feb. 16, 1800, died Feb. 22, 1886.

BIRD. xviii, 10. In memory of our beloved grandparents; Samuel Bird, born Dec. 6, 1785, died Jan. 12, 1866; Catherine Bird, born Feb. 19, 1788, died May 13, 1873.

FELTON. xviii, 11. Rosilla A. Felton died Nov. 15, 1859, aged 2 yrs. 7 mos. 10 days.

FELTON. xviii, 12. Charles C. Felton died Oct. 9, 1864, aged 55 yrs. 10 mos. Horace Felton died March 15, 1865, aged 15 years 10 mos. Mary W., wife of Charles C. Felton, died Feb. 4, 1867, aged 43 yrs. 7 mos.

FISHER. xviii, 13. Here Lyes Buried ye Body of Capt Daniel Fisher, aged about 63 years. Departed This Life Novr ye 17th, 1713.

THORNTON. xviii, 14. Joseph Thornton died Dec. 28, 1870, aged 77 years 29 days. Augustus T. Thornton, a member of Co. B, 4th Reg. R. I. volunteers, Killed at Petersburg, Va., July 30, 1863, aged 24 years.

FIRST PARISH. 47

THORNTON. xviii, 15. Jane A.. wife of Joseph Thornton, died Sept. 12, 1858, aged 59 years 11 mos. & 12 days.

> She sleeps in Jesus, blessed sleep,
> From which none ever wake to weep.

CROSBY. xviii, 16. Obed S., died April 3, 1823, Aet. 3 yrs. & 7 ms. Turana died Sept. 25, 1831, Aet. 17 yrs. Fanny M. died June 2, 1837, Aet. 12 yrs. Mary died April 18, 1843, Aet. 27 yrs. Rhoda, wife of Heman Crosby, died July 27, 1846, Aet. 66 yrs. Heman Crosby died June 18, 1859, Aet. 79 yrs.

HOPKINS. xviii, 17. Capt. Benj. Hopkins died Nov. 12, 1824, Aet. 71. Esther, his wife, died Dec. 5, 1846, Aet. 67.

> Parents we cannot wish you back,
> To this dark world of sin and care,
> To tread with us life's thorny track;
> For you are free from sorrow there.

HOPKINS. xviii, 18. Sacred to the memory of Harriet H. Hopkins, who died April 15, 1841, Aet. 33.

> Here lies a lovely sister dear,
> Sleeping beside her father here;
> Stop, dear friends, & do not weep;
> They are not lost, but gone to sleep.

WOODCOCK. xviii, 19. Here lyes ye Body of Sarah Woodcock, wife to John Woodcock, aged 68 years. Died March ye 18th, 1718.

WOODCOCK. xviii, 20. Here lyes ye Body of John Woodcock, aged 69 years. Died July ye 10th, 1718.

BAKER. xviii, 21. Here lyes ye Body of Mr Nathl Baker, son to Lev^t John & Mrs Sarah Baker, aged 27 years. Dec^d May ye 9th, 1713.

BAKER. xviii, 22. Here lyes interred ye Body of Lieut. John Baker. Departed this life Sept. ye 15th, 1719, in ye 72 year of his age.

BAKER. xviii, 23. Here lyes ye precious dust of Mrs. Abigail Baker, widow of Lieut. John Baker, departed this life Jan^{ry} 14th, 1723, in ye 77th year of her age.

BAKER. xviii, 24. Seth Baker, son to Joseph and Hannah Baker. Died June ye 21, 1720, in the 10th month of his age.

HERRING. xviii, 25. Here lyes ye Body of Mrs. Sarah Herring, wife to James Herring. Dec^d Decr ye 2^d, 1721, in ye 60th year of her age.

SPRAGUE. xviii, 50. Samuel M. Sprague died Jan. 0th, 1841. Aet. 1 yr. 7 ms. Margaret L. Sprague died Sept. 10, 1880. Aet. 2 yrs. 2 ms. Mary, wife of Samuel Sprague, died June 18, 1853. Aet. 41 yrs, 8 ms.

ROBINSON. xviii, 27. Melissa Robinson died Sept. 16, 1842. Aet. 2 yrs. 10 ms. Esther Robinson died Nov. 11, 1852. Aet. 15 ys. 8 ms. Deborah C. Robinson died July 23, 1884. Aet. 72 yrs. 3 ms.

PENNIMAN. xviii, 28. Henry Asa Penniman. Born at Mendon Oct. 24, 1767, died at Milton, Oct. 1, 1854. Aet. 87 yrs. Sally F. Penniman, born at Dedham Nov. 11, 1774, died at Milton Nov. 14, 1860. Aet. 86 years.

PENNIMAN. xviii, 29. James Penniman, 3^d son of Mr. Asa and Mrs. Sally Penniman, died April 17th, 1808, aged 9 months.

> Alas how swift our transient comforts fly,
> And all our pleasures only bloom to die,
> Sweet smiling babe! a spotless flower
> Cut down and withered in an hour.

PENNIMAN. xviii, 30. In memory of George Royal Penniman, son of Mr. Asa and Mrs. Sally Penniman of Boston, who died August 1st, 1801: aged 23 mos. & 7 days.

> Peace to his gentle shade! his soul is free,
> Eased from the pains of sad mortality,
> Enrob'd with innocence, by virtue blessed,
> For Earth too good, he flew to heaven for rest.
>
> Cease then, fond parents, check the rising sigh,
> The child of innocence will never die.
> Hush every fear, lay all your cares to rest,
> Your infant died; he died but to be blest.

STOW. xviii, 31. In memory of Lydia F. Stow, widow of Timothy Stow, jr, who died June 28, 1834, aged 36 years.

> I know that my Redeemer liveth.

STOW. xviii, 32. In memory of Mr. Timothy Stow, jr., who died April 16, 1824, aged 45.

> We mourn the husband and the parent dead,
> The faithful friend and the kind neighbor fled;
> But oh! the nearest, dearest friends must part,
> No more the Tyrant death shall wound his heart.

STOW. xviii, 33. In memory of Edward Stow, who died Aug. 30, 1829: aged 23 years.

> His mind was cast in heavenly mould,
> His-spirit pure now soars above!
> Death never can from God withhold
> The soul; — that trusts in Jesus' love.

POND. xviii, 34. Here lies interred the Body of Mrs Sally Pond, consort of Capt. Eliphalet Pond, who departed this life Jany 1st, 1774, aged 31 years. Likewise two of their children. Viz: Abigail, aged 20, & Sally Aged 21 days.

> Under this stone confin'd doth lie
> Three subjects of Death's Tyranny.
> The mother who in this close tomb
> Sleeps with the offspring of her womb.
> Whereby we see Death's cruelty
> In cutting off both fruit and tree.
> Yet all his malice will prove vain,
> For tree and fruit shall spring again.

DANIELL. xviii, 35. In memory of Mr. Timothy Daniell, son of Jeremiah & Mrs. Abigail Daniell, who died March 19, 1805. Ae. 25.

> Friends nor Physicians could not save,
> My mortal body from the grave.
> Nor can the grave confine it there,
> When Christ shall call me to appear.

STOW. xviii, 36. In memory of Mrs. Betsey Stow, wife of Mr. Timothy Stow, junr, who died April 7th, 1814, aged 31 years.

> Farewell my spouse and children dear
> I've left this world of pain;
> May virtue be your practice here
> Till we do meet again.

DANIELS. xviii, 37. In memory of Mrs. Nabby Daniels, wife of Mr. Joseph Daniels, who died March 7, 1820, aged 36 years.

> Farewell my son and partner dear,
> If aught on earth could keep me here
> 'Twould be my love for you.
> But Jesus calls my soul away;
> Jesus forbids a longer stay.

DANIELL. xviii, 38. Erected by filial love to the memory of a beloved father, Josiah Daniell died April 4, 1816, aged 39 years.

RICHARDS. xviii. 39. In memory of Dea^n Ebenezer Richards, who departed this life Feb. 27th, 1799, Aet. 80 years. In memory of Mrs. Thankful Richards, consort of Dea^n Ebenezer Richards, who departed this life 1 June, 1796, Aet. 76 years.

He performed the office of Deacon in the first church of Dedham for 27 years.

> Blessed are the dead that die in the Lord.

RICHARDS. xviii, 40. Dea. John Richards, Born Aug. 17. 1760, Died July 21, 1837. Sarah Richards, his wife, Born Oct. 26, 1768, Died July 1, 1830.

―― RANGE XIX. ――

DYAR. xix, 1. Here Lyes ye Body of Hannah Dyar, Wife to Benjamin Dyar of Boston, aged 18 years. Dyed Sept. ye 15, 1678. [See page 3.]

MABBETT. xix, 2. Florence Lillian, Daughter of Henry J. & Maria Mabbett. Died Dec. 2. 1875, aged 1 year 8 mo's & 14 days.

> Darling Florrie.
> She is with the angels,
> And we long for her sweet kiss,
> Where the little feet are walking,
> In the realms of perfect bliss.

PARTRIDGE. xix. 3. In memory of two children of Hervey and Rachel Partridge. Angelina died Aug. 26, 1833, aged 16 years. Sarah G. died Jan. 23, 1834. Aged 8 months.

WIGHT. xix, 4. Deacon Joseph Wight, died June 13, 1729. Aet. 75.

WIGHT. xix, 5. Mary Wight, widow of Deacon Joseph Wight, died Dec. 25, 1733. Aet. 73.

CHISHOLM. BARTON. xix, 6. George Chisholm died Oct. 17, 1828, Aet, 1 yr. 6 mos. William Chisholm died June 30, 1808, aged 73 yrs. 11 mos. Isabel Chisholm died June 30, 1808, Aet 74 ys. 4 ms. Mrs. Janet Barton died Nov. 23, 1852, Aet. 26 ys. 9 ms.

GUPTILL. xix, 7. In memory of Lizzie M. Guptill, age 26. Died Mar. 1st, 1876. She is not Dead But Sleepeth.

GRAHAM. xix, 8. Lydia, wife of John Graham & daughter of the late John Curtiss, of Dudley, Mass., died June 6, 1842, Aet. 42. Also Lydia Curtiss, her child, died July 25, Aet. 2 months.

MAYO. xix, 9. James Mayo died Jan 14, 1845. Aet. 66. Abigail, his wife, died April 23, 1854. Aet. 74.

DONLEY. xix, 10. Francis Donley died Ap. 3, 1879, aged 46 years, 3 months, 13 days, Co. I, 35 Reg. Mass. Vols.

HAWS. xix, 11. In memory of Mrs. Sebiah Haws, who died Jan. 16, 1835. Aet. 94.

MORSE, xix, 12. Silas Morse died Jan. 20, 1876, aged 56 yrs. 2 mos. 20 ds. Ruth Stears Morse died Sept. 4, 1882, aged 87 years, 8 mos. 4 ds. Lewis Morse died Oct. 5, 1882, aged 58 ys. 8 ms. 26 d.

DUDLEY. xix, 13. In memory of Miss Harriet, daugh. of Mr. Steph & Mrs. Sybel Dudley, of Readfield, Maine, who died April 19, 1835, aged 25 ys. & 11 ms.

> My flesh shall slumber in the ground,
> Till the last trumpets joyful sound;
> Then burst the chain with sweet surprise
> And in my Savior's image rise.

TALBOT. GUILD. xix, 14. George G., Aug. 28, 1830: 6 mos. Ann S., Sept. 23, 1833; 11 mos. George, Sept. 12, 1839: 9 mos. Children of Sylvester W. & Margaret G. Talbot. We scarce had called them ours.

Sylvester W. Talbot. Aug. 30, 1849. 3 years. Sylvester W. Talbot, April 18, 1847. Aet. 49.

George R. Guild, Sept. 21, 1820. 16 years. Son of Abner & Sophia Guild. Abner Guild, July 6, 1843, aged 70. Sophia H. Guild, Aug. 8, 1858, aged 84. Sophia Guild, Feb. 8, 1867. Aet. 59. Henrietta Guild, Mch. 25, 1874. Aet. 58.

SAMPSON. xix, 15. Mary, wife of Lemuel Sampson, died Feb. 15, 1857. Aet. 93 years. Our mother sleeps.

> Sons and daughters: Such a friend
> For you on earth there lingers not;
> Well may you weep till life shall end.
> Say, can her love be e'er forgot?
> By faith her heavenly march she led,
> And onward pressed whate'er befell;
> By faith she bowed her suffering head
> And sweetly whispered, All is well.

COLBURN. xix, 16. Here lyes ye body of Rebekah Colburn, wife to Benj: Colburn, aged 29 years. Dec^d Jany ye 24, 1723. Annah Colburn, aged 7 weeks, dec^d Aug. ye 27. 1721. Jesse Colburn, aged 6 days, dec^d Jany ye 18th, 1723. John Colburn, aged 6 years, dec^d March ye 5, 1724. Children of Benj^m and Rebekah Colburn.

COLMAN. xix, 17. Benjamin Colman, son of Mr Benjamin & Mⁿ Rebecca Colman. Died March ye 17th, 1731, in the 15 year of His age.

PAUL. SAMPSON. xix, 18. Hiram Paul died Sept. 8, 1873, aged 69 years, 6 mos. Susan B. Paul died June 9, 1888, aged 82 yrs. 22 days. Cynthia Sampson died June 17, 1877, aged 87 yrs. 2 ms, 14 ds.

BISSETT. xix, 19. Charles Bissett died Feb. 11, 1842. Aet. 62 years.

BISSETT. xix, 20. Maria I., wife of Charles Bissett, died April 17, 1879, aged 83 years.

FIRST PARISH. 51

MOODY. xix, 21. Here Lyes Buried y⁰ Body of M⁽ Eliezer Moody, scriv⁽, who departed this life June y⁰ 7ᵗʰ, 1720. ÆTATIS SUÆ 61.

WENTWORTH. CHANDLER. xix, 22. Jason Wentworth died Mar. 11, 1829, Aet. 38. Bethiah Wentworth Born Aug. 22, 1789, died May 2, 1878. Benjamin W. Chandler died Aug. 29, 1848, Aet 2 mos. 6 ds. Eliza Jane, wife of B. Chandler & dau⁽ of J. & B. Wentworth, died July 11, 1856, Aet. 34.

FISHER. xix, 23. Nathaniel, son of Jeremiah and Deborah Fisher, aged about 7 years, Died July, y⁰ 21, 1715.

DWIGHT. xix, 24. Here lyes y⁰ Body of Mary Dwight, wife to Timothy Dwight, aged 49 years. Died August 29, 1689.

HURST. xix, 25. William, son of William & Isabella Hurst, died June 17, 1843, aged 22 mos.

CLARKE. xix, 26. Horatio Clarke, 1810—1873. Elvira R. Clarke, 1813—1881.

WILSON. xix, 27. Here Lyes Buried y⁰ Body of M⁽ Ephraim Wilson, who died Feb⁽ y⁰ 20, 1733, in y⁰ 77ᵗʰ year of His Age.

WILLSON. xix, 28. John Willson, son of M⁽ John M⁽ˢ Hannah Willson, aged 17 months & 4 D⁽. Dec⁽ July y⁰ 17, 1736.

WILLSON. xix, 29. Here Lyes Buried y⁰ Body of M⁽ˢ Anna Willson, wife to M⁽ John Willson, died April 21ˢᵗ, 1737, in y⁰ 24ᵗʰ year of her age. Ebenezer, son to M⁽ John & M⁽ˢ Anna Willson, born & died April 11ᵗʰ, 1737.

BULLARD. xix, 30. In memory of Ens⁰ Isaac Bullard, who died 15ᵗʰ April. 1770, being his birthday, aged 61 years.
In memory of Widow Grace Bullard, who died 26ᵗʰ March, 1789, aged 79 years. Mark the perfect and behold the upright, for their end is peace.

BULLARD. xix, 31. Here Lyes interred the Body of M⁽ˢ Mary Bullard. Late wife of Mr. Isaac Bullard. Aged 34 years 1 month & 18 days. She died Dec⁽ 28ᵗʰ, 1745. The Righteous have Hope in their Death.

WILLSON. xix, 32. Here lyes Buried y⁰ Body of M⁽ˢ Lydia Willson, wife to Mr. Nathˡ Willson, Aged About 54 years. Died Oct. y⁰ 17ᵗʰ, 1740.

BROWN. xix, 33. Charles H. Brown, son of H. C. & O. A. Brown. Died Oct. 17, 1862, Aet. 6 yrs. 3 mo. & 4 days.

WILSON. RICHARDS. xix, 34. Mrs. Esther Wilson, wife of John Wilson, died Sept. 4, 1753, aged 34 years. Mr. John Wilson died May 1, 1788, aged 86 yrs. Mrs. Abigail Wilson, wife of John Wilson, died June 26, 1801, aged 54 yrs. Mr. John Wilson died Sept. 28, 1812, aged 62 years. Miss Maria Osgood died Dec. 1, 1826, aged 26 years. Mrs. Molly Wilson died Oct. 14, 1859, aged 93 years. Maria O., dau⁽ of J. F. & P. I. Wilson, died Oct. 15, 1852, Aet. 32 years. John F. Wilson died July 9, 1853, Aet. 62 years. Polly L., wife of John F. Wilson, died Jan. 18, 1874, Aet. 78 yrs.
Mrs. Abby F. Richards, wife of Luther Richards, died July 30, 1840, aged 22 years. Irving W. Richards, son of Luther & Abby F. Richards, died Aug. 20, 1840, aged 9 weeks.

RICHARDS. xix, 35. In memory of M⁽ˢ Hephzibah Richards, wife of Lieu⁽ Jonathan Richards, who died Nov⁽ 22, 1789, aged 29 years.

> Depart my friend, wipe off your tears,
> Here I must lie till Christ appears.

STOW. xix, 36. In memory of George Stow, son of Mr. Timothy Stow, jr. died July 17, 1814, aged 6 years.

PAINE. xix, 37. Fannie Augusta Paine, Born and Died Dec. 16th, 1858.

GOULD. xix. 38. Sacred to the memory of Doct. John Gould, who died 24 Jan., 1807: aged 46 years.

> How lov'd, how valu'd once avails thee not
> To whom related, or by whom begot,
> A heap of dust alone remains of thee,
> 'Tis all thou art & all the proud shall be.

EVERETT. xix, 39. Affectionately erected by Mrs. Everett to the memory of her Husband, John Everett, jr., who was one of the unfortunate Passengers that perished at the burning of the Steamer Lexington on L. I. Sound on the night of Jan. 13, 1840. Aet. 33.

> Fare thee well thou dear departed Husband
> Rest thou here till Christ shall come,
> Then in Heaven may I but meet thee
> To enjoy a happy home.

NEWELL. xix, 40. In memory of Mr. Ebenezer Newell, who died July 11, 1821. Aged 55.

I am the resurrection and the life; he that believeth in me, though he were dead, yet shall he live.—St. John, xi. 25.

NEWELL. xix, 41. Ebenezer Newell died Oct. 16, 1837. Aet. 33.

Every one which seeth the son and believeth on him may have everlasting life; and I will raise him up at the last day,—John 6: 40.

TOWNSEND. xix, 42. To the Memory of the Revd Jonathan Townsend, A. M., 24 years pastor of the Church of Christ in Medfield, who died of the small pox in the Hospital at Dedham, Dec. 12th, 1776, in the 56th year of his age.

> What can preserve my life, or what destroy?
> An angel's arm can't snatch me from the grave.
> Legions of angels can't confine me there.

BOYNTON. xix, 43. John Boynton died Nov. 2, 1824. Aet. 24. Jesse P. Boynton died Feb. 23, 1825. Aet. 11. Abigail, wife of Luther Boynton, died May 13, 1846. Aet. 73. Luther Boynton died July 24, 1849. Aet. 79.

WHITNEY. SPALDING. xix, 44. Samuel S. Whitney, M. D., died June 30, 1855. Aged 40. Sarah W., only daughter of S. S. and Sarah W. Whitney, Died Sept. 23, 1855, aged 16 months. Dr. Stillman S. Whitney, only son of S. S. & Sarah W. Whitney, Died Nov. 6, 1886, aged 36. Stephen H. Spaulding, M. D., died July 15, 1865, aged 76. Sally, wife of Stephen H. Spaulding, Died June 22, 1882, aged 95 years.

COOLIDGE. xix, 45. Horace. Of such is the Kingdom of Heaven.

BARROWS. xix, 46. Thomas Barrows died May 7, 1880, aged 84 yrs. 9 mos. 1 day. Elizabeth, wife of Thomas Barrows, died Aug. 6, 1860, aged 67 yrs. 6 mos. 20 days. Thomas, son of Thomas and Elizabeth Barrows, died Oct. 29, 1863, aged 38 yrs. 7 mos. 22 days. Edward Barrows died Feb. 1, 1881, 52 yrs. 6 mos.

RICHARDS. xix, 47. In memory of Mrs. Elizabeth Richards, wife of Abiathar Richards, who died Aug. 3d, 1814, aged 84 years.

> Blessed are the dead that die in the Lord.

RICHARDS. xix, 48, In memory of Mr. Abiathar Richards who died Sept. 30, 1803, aged 73 years.

Ye living men, come view the ground,
Where you must shortly lie.

RICHARDS. xix, 49. In memory of Elizabeth Richards, dau. of Mr. Abiathar & Mrs. Elizabeth Richards, who died 11 Oct'r, 1802, aged 18 months.

GAY. xix, 50. Jotham Gay died May 17, 1848, Aet. 57.

RICHARDS. xix, 51. In memory of Eliphalet, son of Mr. Abiathar & Mrs. Elizabeth Richards, who Died Sept. 21st, 1792, in ye 18th year of his age.

GAY. xix, 52. In memory of Mrs. Lydia Gay, wife of Mr. Jotham Gay, who died Jan. 6th, 1820, aged 25 years.

Farewell, my spouse, and children dear,
I've left this world of pain;
May virtue be your practice here
Till we do meet again.

BONNEMORT. TYLER. xix, 53. Nicholas Bonnemort died Nov. 3, 1885, aged 85 yrs. 3 mos. 7 D. Mary Gill, wife of N. Bonnemort, died May 4, 1856, aged 46 yrs. 7 mo.

Nicholas M. died July 22, 1837, aged 2 yrs. 7 mos. Maratio N, Geo. P. Children of N. and M. Bonnemort. Mariatho N. Bonnemort died Aug. 22, 1802, aged 48 years.

Mrs. Eunice Tyler died Apr. 22, 1824, aged 45 years.

RICHARDS. xix, 54. In memory of Mrs. Mary Richards, consort of Mr. Job Richards, who died June 7th, 1797, in y^e 66 year of her age.

[*Note.*—This double stone was broken by a falling tree, but on the footstone under the name of Mr. Job Richards, is the date 1798.—C. S.]

www.ingramcontent.com/pod-product-compliance
Lightning Source LLC
LaVergne TN
LVHW051712080426
835511LV00017B/2863